Contents

Beef and walnut loaf

Overall timing 1 hour

Freezing Suitable

To serve 6

2	Onions	2
2	Tomatoes	2
$1\frac{1}{2}$ lb	Stewing beef	700g
2oz	Walnuts	50g
1 teasp	Paprika	5ml
	Salt and pepper	
2	Eggs	2

Preheat oven to 400°F (200°C) Gas 6.

Peel and roughly chop the onions. Blanch and peel the tomatoes. Wipe and trim the stewing beef and put through the mincer with the onions and tomatoes. Put mixture in a bowl.

Finely chop walnuts and add to bowl with paprika, salt, pepper and eggs. Mix well. Shape into a mound, place on a greased baking tray and flatten the top slightly.

Bake for 15 minutes, then reduce temperature to 350°F (180°C) Gas 4 and bake for a further 35 minutes, till firm and well browned.

Serve cut into wedges, with creamed potatoes and courgettes, or with jacket potatoes and coleslaw.

SUPPERS & SNACKS

Edited by Norma MacMillan and Wendy James
Home economist Gilly Cubitt

ORBIS PUBLISHING London

Introduction

These delicious suppers and snacks provide the perfect answer when a full-scale meal is not wanted. They vary from sandwiches and hearty soups to mouth-watering pasta and meat dishes, and many can be prepared very quickly or just reheated from the freezer.

Both imperial and metric measures are given for each recipe; you should follow only one set of measures as they are not direct conversions. All spoon measures are level unless otherwise stated. Pastry quantities are based on the amount of flour used. Dried herbs may be substituted for fresh herbs: use one-third of the quantity.

Photographs were supplied by Editions Atlas, Editions Atlas/Cedus, Editions Atlas/Masson, Editions Atlas/Zadora, Archivio IGDA, Lavinia Press Agency, Orbis GmbH, Wales Tourist Board

The material in this book has previously appeared in *The Complete Cook*

First published 1981 in Great Britain by Orbis Publishing Limited, 20–22 Bedfordbury, London WC2

ISBN 0-85613-368-X
Printed in Singapore

Danish meatballs

Overall timing 40 minutes

Freezing Suitable: fry meatballs after thawing, or fry from frozen, allowing 25 minutes

To serve 4

4oz	Fresh breadcrumbs	125g
¼ pint	Milk	150ml
1	Small onion	1
8oz	Minced beef	225g
8oz	Minced pork	225g
	Salt and pepper	
½ teasp	Ground allspice	2.5ml
1	Egg	1
2 tbsp	Plain flour	2x15ml
2oz	Butter	50g
3 tbsp	Oil	3x15ml
8	Lettuce leaves	8
2	Pickled beetroot	2
4 tbsp	Pickled red cabbage	4x15ml

Put fresh breadcrumbs into a bowl with the milk and soak for 10 minutes.

Peel onion and grate into a large bowl. Add the beef and pork, squeezed out breadcrumbs, salt, pepper and allspice. Mix well and bind together with the beaten egg. Shape mixture into eight balls and coat lightly with flour.

Heat butter and oil in a frying pan. Add meatballs and fry gently for 15 minutes till brown all over and cooked through.

Meanwhile, wash and dry lettuce leaves and arrange in a shallow basket or serving dish. Drain and dice pickled beetroot.

Remove meatballs from pan with a draining spoon and drain on kitchen paper. Put one meatball on each lettuce leaf and spoon a little drained pickled cabbage and beetroot around. Serve with a lettuce, tomato and olive salad.

Corned beef patties

Overall timing 30 minutes

Freezing Suitable: cook from frozen

To serve 4

12 tbsp	Fresh breadcrumbs	12x15 ml
3 tbsp	Warm milk	3x15 ml
1 lb	Corned beef	450 g
2	Eggs	2
2 tbsp	Grated Parmesan cheese	2x15 ml
	Grated rind of ½ lemon	
	Plain flour	
2 oz	Butter	50 g
1 tbsp	Oil	15 ml
	Lemon wedges	
	Sprigs of parsley	

Soak 4 tbsp (4x15 ml) breadcrumbs in the milk. Cut off any excess fat from the edge of the corned beef and discard. Mash beef in a bowl with a fork, then add squeezed-out breadcrumbs, 1 egg, the cheese and lemon rind. Mix well.

With well floured hands, make patties from the mixture, then coat with flour. Lightly beat remaining egg. Using two forks, dip the patties first into beaten egg, then into remaining breadcrumbs.

Heat butter and oil in a large frying pan. Add the patties and cook over a moderate heat till brown on both sides. Remove from pan and drain on kitchen paper. Garnish with lemon wedges and parsley.

Kidneys in their jackets

Overall timing 45 minutes

Freezing Not suitable

To serve 4

8	Lamb kidneys in their suet	8
4	Slices of bread	4
	Salt and pepper	
1	Tomato	1
	Sprigs of parsley	

Preheat the oven to 400°F (200°C) Gas 6.

Place kidneys in their suet in a roasting tin. Bake for about 35 minutes till the fat is crisp and golden.

Pour a little of the melted fat from the roasting tin into a frying pan and fry the bread till golden on both sides. Arrange slices in warmed individual dishes.

Cut a deep cross in the top of the kidneys and open out like petals. Season inside and place on top of fried bread. Wash tomatoes and cut into wedges. Arrange with parsley sprigs on top of kidneys. Serve with sauté or mashed potatoes.

Porkburgers

Overall timing 25 minutes

Freezing Suitable: cook from frozen

To serve 6

$1\frac{1}{2}$ lb	Lean pork	700g
	Salt and pepper	
1	Onion	1
1 teasp	Dried thyme	5ml
1 tbsp	Oil	15ml
	Lemon slices	

Mince the pork twice till fine and add plenty of salt and pepper. Peel and finely chop the onion and add to the pork with the dried thyme. Mix well with a wooden spoon.

Divide the meat into six portions and shape into thick burgers about 4 inches (10cm) in diameter.

Brush a heavy-based frying pan or griddle with oil and heat well. Add the burgers and fry for about 10–15 minutes. Turn burgers carefully with a fish slice and cook for a further 5–10 minutes according to taste.

Garnish with lemon slices and serve with an endive and tomato salad or with chips.

Chicken parcels

Overall timing 45 minutes

Freezing Suitable: bake from frozen, allowing 35–45 minutes

To serve 6		
13 oz	Frozen puff pastry	375 g
1	Medium-size onion	1
1 oz	Butter	25 g
10 oz	Cooked boneless chicken	275 g
3 tbsp	Chopped parsley	3x15 ml
4 tbsp	Double cream	4x15 ml
	Salt and pepper	
3	Slices of cooked ham	3
1	Egg yolk	1
6	Lettuce leaves	6

Thaw pastry. Preheat oven to 400°F (200°C) Gas 6.

Peel and chop onion and fry in the butter till transparent.

Set aside six fairly large pieces of chicken and finely chop the rest. Put chopped chicken into a bowl with the parsley and fried onion. Lightly beat the cream, then stir into the chicken with seasoning.

Roll out the dough on a lightly floured surface. Cut out six 5 inch (12.5 cm) squares. Cut ham slices in half and place one piece in centre of each dough square. Top with a piece of chicken, then cover with chopped chicken mixture. Dampen dough edges with cold water. Fold corners to centre to cover the filling, pinching the edges together, but leaving a small hole in the top. Place parcels on a greased baking tray.

Beat the egg yolk with a pinch of salt and brush over parcels. Bake for 25 minutes or until well risen and golden brown. Serve the parcels on lettuce leaves.

Ham and potato cake

Overall timing $1\frac{1}{4}$ hours

Freezing Not suitable

To serve 4

$1\frac{1}{2}$ lb	Medium-size potatoes	700 g
	Salt and pepper	
8 oz	Sliced cooked ham	225 g
8 oz	Cheese	225 g
3 oz	Butter	75 g
3 tbsp	Fresh breadcrumbs	3x15 ml
$\frac{1}{4}$ pint	Milk	150 ml

Cook potatoes in boiling salted water for 20 minutes.

Meanwhile, chop the ham and grate cheese. Grease a 7 inch (18 cm) springform tin with a little of the butter and sprinkle breadcrumbs over the bottom and sides, shaking off any excess. Preheat oven to 350°F (180°C) Gas 4.

Drain and peel the potatoes, then cut into $\frac{1}{4}$ inch (6 mm) thick slices. Arrange a few of the slices, slightly overlapping, in the bottom of the tin. Melt the remaining butter and brush a little over the potatoes. Scatter some of the ham, then some of the cheese over and season. Continue layering, reserving a little of the butter, and finishing with a layer of potato topped with cheese. Pour the milk over and brush with remaining butter.

Bake for about 30 minutes till potatoes are tender and cheese has melted. Turn cake out of tin to serve.

Brazilian meat pasties

Overall timing 50 minutes

Freezing Suitable: omit hard-boiled eggs and bake from frozen in 425°F (220°C) Gas 7 oven for 30 minutes

To serve 4		
13 oz	Frozen puff pastry	375 g
1	Onion	1
4 oz	Belly pork rashers	125 g
1 oz	Butter	25 g
8 oz	Minced beef	225 g
3 tbsp	Seedless raisins	3x15 ml
	Pinch of ground cloves	
	Salt and pepper	
$\frac{1}{4}$ teasp	Paprika	1.25 ml
2	Hard-boiled eggs	2
8	Stoned green olives	8
1	Egg	1

Thaw the pastry. Roll out to a rectangle 8x16 inches (20x40 cm). Cut into eight 4 inch (10 cm) squares.

Preheat oven to 400°F (200°C) Gas 6.

Peel and finely chop the onion. Derind and mince the belly pork rashers. Melt the butter in a frying pan and fry the onion and pork till golden. Add the minced beef and fry briskly, stirring frequently, till brown.

Remove from heat and add the raisins, cloves, salt, pepper and paprika. Mix well. Shell and coarsely chop the hard-boiled eggs. Chop the olives, add to the pan with the eggs and mix well.

Place one eighth of the meat mixture on half of each dough square. Brush the edges with a little of the beaten egg and fold dough over. Crimp edges to seal.

Arrange on a dampened baking tray and brush tops with beaten egg. Bake for about 25 minutes till well risen and golden.

Pork and beans

Overall timing $2\frac{3}{4}$ hours plus overnight soaking

Freezing Not suitable

To serve 4

1 lb	Dried butter beans	450 g
1	Onion	1
12	Cloves	12
2	Garlic cloves	2
$2\frac{1}{2}$ pints	Boiling water	1.5 litres
4 tbsp	Oil	4x15 ml
	Salt and pepper	
1 lb	Piece of smoked streaky bacon or belly of pork	450 g

Put the beans in a large saucepan of cold water and soak overnight.

The next day, bring to the boil and cook beans for 15 minutes. Drain.

Peel onion, spike with the cloves and add to pan with peeled garlic, boiling water, oil, pepper and bacon or belly pork, derinded and cut into thick rashers if easier to handle. Cover and simmer for $1\frac{1}{2}$ hours. Taste and add salt, then cook for a further 30 minutes.

Remove spiked onion and garlic. Remove meat and beans from pan with a draining spoon and place in warmed serving dish. Keep hot.

Reduce cooking liquor to about $\frac{1}{4}$ pint (150 ml) by boiling fast, uncovered. Pour over beans and serve.

Frankfurter fritters

Overall timing 30 minutes

Freezing Not suitable

To serve 6

5 oz	Plain flour	150 g
	Salt and pepper	
1	Egg	1
1 tbsp	Oil	15 ml
4 fl oz	Beer	120 ml
	Oil for frying	
16	Frankfurters	16
2	Egg whites	2

Sift 4 oz (125 g) of the flour into a bowl with $1\frac{1}{2}$ teasp (7.5 ml) salt and make a well in the centre. Add the whole egg and oil and mix with a wooden spoon. Gradually add the beer and mix to a smooth batter.

Heat the oil in a deep-fryer to 340°F (170°C).

Season the remaining flour. Cut the frankfurters in half and toss in flour. Whisk the egg whites till stiff but not dry and fold into the batter. Dip each frankfurter half into the batter and fry in the oil for about 3 minutes till crisp and golden. Drain on kitchen paper and serve hot.

Bacon and apple rings

Overall timing 40 minutes

Freezing Not suitable

To serve 4		
8 oz	Thin streaky bacon rashers	225 g
1 oz	Butter	25 g
2	Yellow Golden Delicious apples	2
2 tbsp	Caster sugar	2x15 ml

Derind the bacon. Melt the butter in a frying pan, add the bacon and fry till crisp. Drain on kitchen paper, place on a warmed serving plate and keep hot.

Wash, dry and core apples, but don't peel them. Cut into thin rings and cook in the frying pan till tender, turning them over with a spatula. Drain on kitchen paper, then arrange on the serving plate with the bacon.

Sprinkle with sugar and serve immediately with hot toast and butter.

Spanish kebabs

Overall timing 25 minutes plus marination

Freezing Not suitable

To serve 4		
1 lb	Thick white fish fillets	450 g
2 tbsp	Oil	2x15 ml
2 tbsp	Lemon juice	2x15 ml
	Salt and pepper	
8 oz	Garlic sausage	225 g
8	Smoked streaky bacon rashers	8
16	Bay leaves	16
3 oz	Butter	75 g

Cut the fish into 16 neat cubes and put into a bowl with the oil, half the lemon juice and salt and pepper. Marinate for 1 hour, turning occasionally.

Preheat the grill and line the pan with foil. Cut the sausage into $\frac{1}{2}$ inch (12.5 mm) slices. Derind and stretch the bacon rashers and cut each in half. Thread the fish cubes, sausage, bay leaves and folded bacon on to greased skewers.

Place on the grill pan and brush the marinade over. Grill for about 10 minutes, turning and basting frequently, till the fish is tender.

Melt the butter in a saucepan and add the remaining lemon juice and seasoning. Serve this sauce with the kebabs.

Fishermen's herrings

Overall timing 35 minutes plus chilling

Freezing Not suitable

To serve 6

12	Smoked herring fillets	12
1	Onion	1
4	Small gherkins	4
4oz	Can of herring roes	113g
1 tbsp	French mustard	15ml
$\frac{1}{4}$ pint	Oil	150ml
	Pepper	

Put the herring fillets into a bowl, cover with boiling water and leave for 20 minutes.

Drain herring fillets, rinse and dry on kitchen paper. Peel onion and cut into thin rings. Slice gherkins.

Drain and chop the roes and put into a bowl with the mustard. Beat to a smooth paste with a wooden spoon. Gradually trickle in all but 2 tbsp (2x15ml) of the oil, beating well after each addition. Add pepper to taste.

Spread roe sauce over bottom of a serving dish and arrange herring fillets on top. Brush with remaining oil and decorate with onion rings and gherkins. Chill for at least 30 minutes, then serve with potato and beetroot salads garnished with snipped chives.

Cod croquettes

Overall timing 45 minutes

Freezing Suitable: bake cooked croquettes from frozen in 375°F (190°C) Gas 5 oven for 30 minutes

To serve 4–6		
1 lb	Cooked cod fillets	450g
1 lb	Mashed potatoes	450g
	Salt and pepper	
	Grated nutmeg	
1	Egg	1
	Dried breadcrumbs	
	Oil for deep frying	
	Lettuce leaves	
1	Lemon	1

Finely mince cod, then mix with potatoes in a large bowl. Season well with salt, pepper and a pinch of nutmeg. Make small round or oval shapes of the mixture.

Lightly beat egg in a bowl. Dip croquettes in egg, then breadcrumbs.

Heat oil in deep-fryer to 360°F (180°C). Add croquettes and fry for about 5 minutes till golden. Remove croquettes and drain on kitchen paper. Pile them up on a bed of lettuce with pieces of lemon between. Serve with tomato sauce (see page 19).

Pasta and rice

Meatball lasagne

Overall timing 3 hours

Freezing Suitable: bake, covered, from frozen in 350°F (180°C) Gas 4 oven for 1½ hours; remove cover for last 30 minutes to brown top

To serve 6

2	Onions	2
4 oz	Streaky bacon	125 g
6 tbsp	Oil	6x15 ml
1 lb	Chuck steak	450 g
14 oz	Can of tomatoes	397 g
½ pint	Stock	300 ml
	Salt and pepper	
12 oz	Lasagne	350 g
2 tbsp	Chopped parsley	2x15 ml
1	Egg	1
3 oz	Grated Parmesan cheese	75 g
3 tbsp	Plain flour	3x15 ml
4 oz	Cooked ham	125 g
4 oz	Mozzarella cheese	125 g

Peel and chop onions. Derind and chop bacon. Heat 3 tbsp (3x15 ml) oil in a saucepan, add onions and bacon and cook till golden. Add steak and brown on all sides. Add tomatoes, stock and seasoning. Cover and cook for 1½–2 hours till meat is tender. Lift steak out of pan, reserving sauce, and cool.

Cook lasagne in boiling salted water for 15–20 minutes till tender. Drain.

Mince steak, then mix with parsley, egg, half Parmesan and seasoning. Roll into small balls and toss in seasoned flour. Heat remaining oil in a frying pan and brown meatballs all over. Drain on kitchen paper.

Preheat oven to 400°F (200°C) Gas 6.

Dice ham and Mozzarella. Reserve 3 tbsp (3x15 ml) Parmesan. Layer lasagne, ham, cheeses, meatballs and sauce in greased roasting tin, ending with reserved Parmesan. Bake for 35 minutes.

Spaghetti with tomato sauce

Overall timing 30 minutes

Freezing Not suitable

To serve 4

1	Onion	1
2 lb	Cherry or plum tomatoes	900 g
	Bouquet garni	
	Pinch of sugar	
	Cayenne pepper or Tabasco sauce	
	Salt and pepper	
1 tbsp	Chopped fresh basil or parsley	15 ml
12 oz	Spaghetti	350 g

Peel and chop the onion. Halve the tomatoes. Put the onion and tomatoes in a saucepan with the bouquet garni and simmer gently until mushy.

Discard the bouquet garni, then rub the tomato sauce through a sieve, or purée in a blender. Return to the pan and add the sugar, a little cayenne or Tabasco sauce and seasoning. Stir in the herbs and reheat gently.

Meanwhile, cook the spaghetti in boiling salted water till just tender. Drain well and turn into a warmed serving dish. Pile the tomato sauce on top and serve.

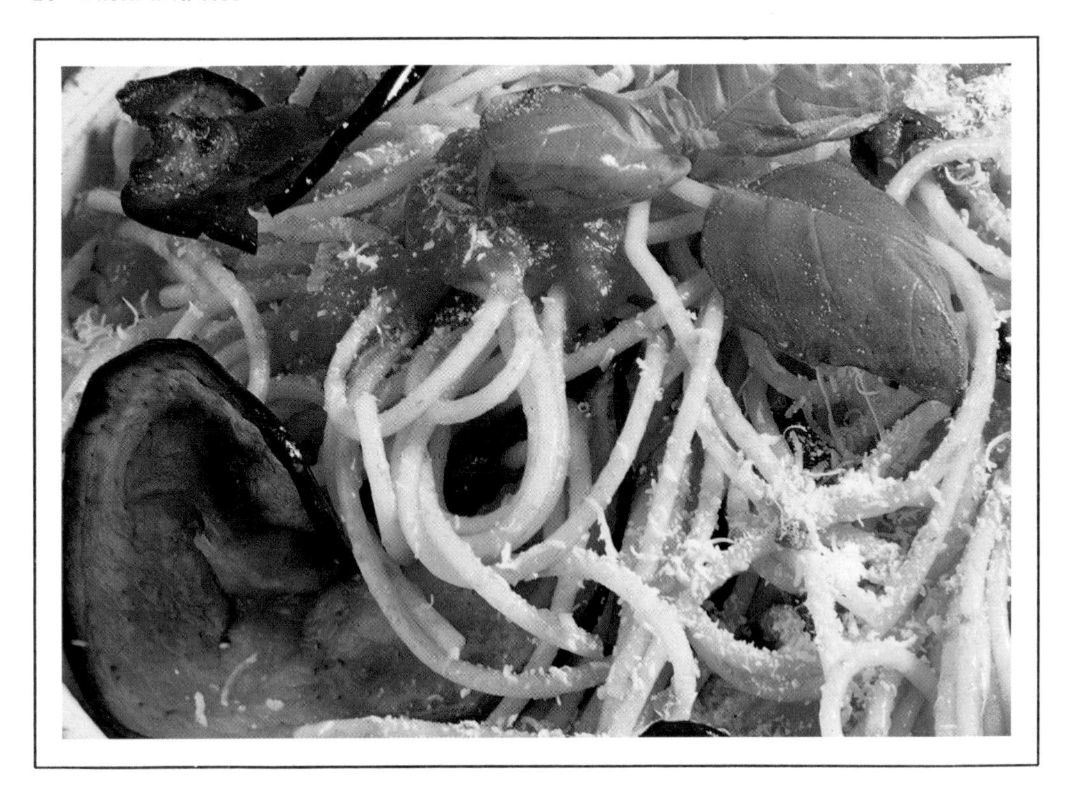

Spaghetti with aubergines

Overall timing 45 minutes plus draining

Freezing Not suitable

To serve 4

1	Large aubergine	1
	Salt and pepper	
1 lb	Ripe tomatoes	450 g
1	Garlic clove	1
	Oil	
2 teasp	Chopped fresh basil	2x5 ml
12 oz	Spaghetti	350 g
2 oz	Grated Parmesan cheese	50 g
	Sprig of basil	

Wash and thinly slice the aubergine. Put into a colander and sprinkle with salt. Leave to drain for 1 hour.

Blanch, peel and chop the tomatoes. Peel and crush garlic. Heat 3 tbsp (3x15 ml) oil in a saucepan, add garlic and fry for 1 minute. Add tomatoes, basil and seasoning, stir well and cook over a low heat for 15 minutes.

Cook spaghetti in boiling salted water till tender.

Meanwhile, rinse aubergine slices under running water and gently squeeze dry. Heat ½ inch (12.5 mm) oil in a frying pan and fry aubergine slices, a few at a time, till crisp on both sides. Drain on kitchen paper and keep hot.

Drain spaghetti thoroughly. Put into a warmed serving dish and pour tomato sauce over. Add aubergine slices, sprinkle with cheese, garnish with sprig of basil and serve.

Neapolitan cannelloni

Overall timing $1\frac{1}{2}$ hours

Freezing Suitable: reheat from frozen in 350°F (180°C) Gas 4 oven for 1 hour

To serve 4		
12	Sheets of lasagne	12
8oz	Mozzarella cheese	225g
2oz	Cooked ham	50g
8oz	Cream cheese	225g
2	Eggs	2
	Salt and pepper	
$1\frac{1}{2}$oz	Grated Parmesan cheese	40g
Tomato sauce		
1	Onion	1
1	Garlic clove	1
1 tbsp	Oil	15ml
14oz	Can of tomatoes	397g
1 tbsp	Chopped fresh basil	15ml

Cook lasagne in boiling salted water for 10–15 minutes till tender. Drain and spread on a damp cloth to cool.

Thinly slice the Mozzarella. Dice ham. Place in a bowl with the cream cheese, eggs and seasoning. Mix well.

For the sauce, peel and finely chop onion. Peel and crush garlic. Heat oil in a saucepan, add onion and garlic and fry until golden. Add tomatoes in their juice, basil, salt and pepper. Cook for 10 minutes, stirring occasionally.

Preheat oven to 425°F (220°C) Gas 7.

Divide cheese mixture between lasagne sheets. Roll lasagne around filling and arrange, joins down, in greased ovenproof dish. Pour over the tomato sauce. Sprinkle half the Parmesan on top and bake for 15 minutes or until golden. Sprinkle with the rest of the Parmesan and serve immediately.

Striped vermicelli

Overall timing 45 minutes

Freezing Not suitable

To serve 4

1	Can of anchovies	1
6 tbsp	Milk	6x15 ml
1	Large onion	1
1	Garlic clove	1
2 tbsp	Oil	2x15 ml
14 oz	Can of tomatoes	397 g
	Salt and pepper	
	Chilli powder	
1 tbsp	Chopped parsley	15 ml
12 oz	Vermicelli	350 g
$\frac{1}{4}$ pint	Carton of double cream	150 ml

Drain the anchovies and soak in the milk for 10 minutes.

Meanwhile, peel and finely chop the onion; peel and crush the garlic. Heat the oil in a small saucepan, add onion and garlic and fry till transparent. Add tomatoes and juice, salt, a pinch of chilli powder and parsley. Simmer for 20 minutes, stirring frequently.

Drain the anchovies and add to the tomato mixture. Purée in a blender or rub through a sieve. Season and reheat gently.

Cook the vermicelli in boiling salted water for 3 minutes till tender. Drain thoroughly and arrange on a warmed flat serving dish. Smooth the top and keep hot.

Warm the cream, then spread it in a wide band across the centre of the vermicelli. Spread the tomato sauce in a wide band on either side of the cream. Serve with hot garlic bread.

Seafood spaghetti

Overall timing 20 minutes

Freezing Not suitable

To serve 4

12 oz	Spaghetti	350 g
	Salt and pepper	
1	Garlic clove	1
3 tbsp	Oil	3x15 ml
8 oz	Large shelled prawns	225 g
10 oz	Can of baby clams or mussels	280 g
8 oz	Can of tomatoes	227 g
1 tbsp	Chopped parsley	15 ml

Cook spaghetti in boiling salted water till tender.

Meanwhile, peel and crush garlic. Heat oil in a large saucepan, add garlic and fry for 1 minute. Add prawns and fry, stirring, for 2–3 minutes.

Drain clams or mussels and add to pan with tomatoes and their juice and seasoning. Cook for about 3 minutes, stirring to break up tomatoes.

Drain spaghetti thoroughly. Add to seafood sauce with parsley and toss lightly over a low heat till well coated. Serve immediately.

Spinach ravioli

Overall timing 1¼ hours

Freezing Suitable: cook ravioli from frozen, then add to tomato sauce

To serve 4–6

12oz	Strong flour	350g
	Salt and pepper	
3	Eggs	3
2	Bacon rashers	2
1	Large onion	1
1	Garlic clove	1
1 tbsp	Oil	15ml
4oz	Minced veal	125g
4oz	Sausagemeat	125g
¼ teasp	Grated nutmeg	1.25ml
6 tbsp	Dry white wine	6x15ml
1lb	Spinach	450g
14oz	Can of tomatoes	397g
2oz	Butter	50g

Sift flour and 1 teasp (5ml) salt into a bowl. Add eggs and mix to smooth, glossy dough.

Derind and dice bacon. Peel and finely chop onion; peel and crush garlic. Heat oil in a saucepan, add bacon, onion and garlic and fry for 5 minutes. Add the veal, sausagemeat and nutmeg and fry for 5 minutes. Stir in wine and seasoning and bring to the boil. Cover and simmer for 15 minutes.

Shred spinach and add to meat. Cover and simmer for a further 5 minutes.

Roll out dough to a large rectangle. Cut out rounds. Dot spoonfuls of spinach mixture on rounds. Fold in half and pinch edges to seal. Roll each half-moon round your forefinger and pinch ends together.

Cook ravioli in boiling salted water till tender. Drain. Press tomatoes through a sieve. Melt butter in pan, stir in tomatoes and seasoning and heat. Return ravioli to pan and toss lightly till coated.

Crisp-topped macaroni with tuna

Overall timing 35 minutes

Freezing Not suitable

To serve 4

1	Onion	1
3oz	Butter	75g
¼ pint	Chicken stock	150ml
	Salt and pepper	
1	Medium cauliflower	1
8oz	Short-cut macaroni	225g
6	Anchovy fillets	6
1oz	Fresh breadcrumbs	25g
7oz	Can of tuna	198g
4 tbsp	Grated Parmesan cheese	4x15ml

Peel and chop the onion. Melt 1oz (25g) of the butter in a large saucepan and fry the onion till golden. Add the chicken stock and seasoning. Bring to the boil and simmer for 5 minutes.

Divide cauliflower into florets and cook in boiling salted water for 4 minutes. Remove with a draining spoon and reserve. Add macaroni to boiling water and cook till tender.

Meanwhile, melt remaining butter in a frying pan and fry cauliflower till golden. Roughly chop anchovies and add to pan with breadcrumbs. Fry till crisp. Remove from heat.

Preheat the grill.

Drain the macaroni and add to the stock mixture. Drain and flake tuna and stir carefully into the macaroni with half the Parmesan. Taste and adjust seasoning and heat through gently.

Pour the macaroni mixture into a flameproof dish and scatter cauliflower and breadcrumb mixture over it. Sprinkle with remaining cheese, then grill for 5 minutes till golden.

Stuffed rigatoni

Overall timing 1 hour

Freezing Not suitable

To serve 4

2	Potatoes	2
4oz	Button mushrooms	125g
2 tbsp	Oil	2x15ml
12oz	Finely minced beef	350g
1 tbsp	Plain flour	15ml
2 tbsp	Dry white wine	2x15ml
½ pint	Beef stock	300ml
2 teasp	Tomato purée	2x5ml
	Salt and pepper	
12oz	Large rigatoni	350g
1	Egg	1
	Tomato sauce (see page 19)	
2 tbsp	Grated Parmesan cheese	2x15ml
½oz	Butter	15g

Peel and grate potatoes. Thinly slice mushrooms. Heat oil in large saucepan, add mushrooms and minced beef and fry for 5 minutes, stirring. Sprinkle in the flour and cook for another 2 minutes. Gradually stir in wine and stock and bring to the boil. Stir in tomato purée, grated potatoes and seasoning. Cover and simmer gently for 20 minutes, stirring occasionally.

Meanwhile, cook rigatoni in boiling salted water till tender. Drain, rinse and spread on a damp tea-towel.

Preheat oven to 350°F (180°C) Gas 4.

Remove the beef mixture from heat and allow to cool a little before beating in the egg. When cool enough to handle, place in a piping bag and pipe carefully into rigatoni. Arrange stuffed rigatoni in greased ovenproof dish.

Pour tomato sauce over and sprinkle with Parmesan. Dot with butter and bake for 15 minutes till bubbling hot.

Cheesy noodles with ham

Overall timing 1 hour

Freezing Not suitable

To serve 4

8 oz	Tagliatelle	225 g
	Salt and pepper	
4 oz	Cheese	125 g
3	Eggs	3
$\frac{3}{4}$ pint	White sauce	400 ml
4 oz	Sliced cooked ham	125 g

Preheat the oven to 400°F (200°C) Gas 6.

Cook the noodles in boiling salted water for about 10 minutes till tender.

Grate cheese. Separate eggs. Stir yolks, 3 oz (75 g) of the cheese and seasoning into sauce.

Cut ham into strips and stir into the sauce. Drain noodles thoroughly and fold into sauce. Season to taste. Whisk the egg whites in a bowl till stiff but not dry and fold into the mixture with metal spoon.

Pour the mixture into a greased ovenproof dish. Sprinkle remaining grated cheese over and bake for about 30 minutes till set and golden. Serve immediately with whole green beans mixed with flaked almonds and butter.

Macaroni with mushrooms

Overall timing 30 minutes

Freezing Not suitable

To serve 4

4oz	Button mushrooms	125g
4oz	Butter	125g
8fl oz	Carton of single cream	227ml
12oz	Short-cut macaroni	350g
	Salt and pepper	
4oz	Cooked ham	125g
2oz	Grated Parmesan cheese	50g
½ pint	White sauce	300ml

Finely chop the mushrooms. Place in a small saucepan with 2oz (50g) of the butter and cook gently for 5 minutes. Remove from heat and stir in cream.

Cook macaroni in boiling salted water till tender. Drain.

Cut the ham into pieces and add to the macaroni with 1oz (25g) of cheese, 1oz (25g) of butter and seasoning. Place macaroni in a flameproof dish with mushroom mixture and stir well. Cook gently for 10 minutes.

Preheat grill.

Pour white sauce over macaroni, sprinkle with remaining cheese and dot with remaining butter. Grill for 5 minutes.

Lasagne col pesto

Overall timing 1 hour

Freezing Suitable: reheat, covered with foil, in 350°F (180°C) Gas 4 oven for 1 hour

To serve 4

12oz	Lasagne	350g
	Salt	
4 tbsp	Grated Parmesan cheese	4x15 ml
2oz	Butter	50g
Pesto		
2	Garlic cloves	2
4 tbsp	Chopped fresh basil	4x15 ml
4 tbsp	Olive oil	4x15 ml
1oz	Grated Parmesan cheese	25g
	Pinch of salt	

Cook the lasagne in boiling salted water for 15–20 minutes till tender. Drain thoroughly and spread out on a damp cloth to cool.

Preheat oven to 350°F (180°C) Gas 4.

To make the pesto, peel and chop garlic and put in mortar with basil. Pound with pestle, gradually adding oil, Parmesan and salt.

Spread one-third of the lasagne over the bottom of a greased ovenproof dish. Spread with one-third of the pesto and sprinkle over 1 tbsp (15 ml) Parmesan. Repeat layers twice, adding extra Parmesan to the top. Dot with butter and bake for 20 minutes till heated through.

Crusty noodle shapes

Overall timing 55 minutes

Freezing Not suitable

To serve 4

12oz	Egg noodles	350g
	Salt	
1oz	Cheese	25g
$\frac{3}{4}$ pint	White sauce	400ml
$\frac{1}{4}$ teasp	Grated nutmeg	1.25ml
2	Eggs	2
1oz	Dried breadcrumbs	25g
6 tbsp	Oil	6x15ml
4oz	Sliced cooked ham	125g
4oz	Mozzarella cheese	125g
	Sprigs of parsley	
	Lemon	

Cook the noodles in boiling salted water for about 5 minutes till tender. Drain the noodles thoroughly and put into a bowl.

Grate the cheese and mix into the white sauce with nutmeg. Pour the sauce over the noodles and mix well. Press into a roasting tin to 1 inch (2.5cm) thickness and leave to cool.

Preheat the oven to 450°F (230°C) Gas 8.

Beat the eggs in a bowl with salt. Spread the breadcrumbs on a sheet of greaseproof paper.

Cut the noodle mixture into diamond shapes or rounds with a biscuit cutter. Dip the shapes into the egg, then the breadcrumbs, pressing the crumbs on to the shapes to make them stick. Heat the oil in a frying pan and fry the shapes until golden on both sides. Drain on kitchen paper. Using a sharp knife, slice each one through the centre.

Halve each slice of ham and put a piece on the bottom half of each shape; top with a thin slice of Mozzarella. Replace the top half of each shape and arrange on a baking tray. Bake for about 10 minutes. Serve hot, garnished with parsley sprigs and lemon.

Spaghetti with piquant sauce

Overall timing 50 minutes

Freezing Not suitable

To serve 4

1	Can of anchovy fillets	1
4 tbsp	Milk	4x15 ml
1 lb	Ripe tomatoes	450 g
1	Garlic clove	1
1	Dried red chilli	1
3 fl oz	Olive oil	90 ml
1 tbsp	Tomato purée	15 ml
2 tbsp	Capers	2x15 ml
12 oz	Spaghetti	350 g
	Salt and pepper	
4 oz	Stoned black olives	125 g

Drain the anchovies and put into a small bowl with the milk. Soak for 10 minutes. Blanch, peel and chop the tomatoes. Peel and crush the garlic; deseed and finely chop the chilli.

Heat the oil in a saucepan, add the garlic and cook for 2 minutes. Drain the anchovies, discarding the milk. Chop and add to the pan with the chilli. Fry for 3 minutes, pressing the anchovies with the back of a wooden spoon to break them up.

Add the tomatoes, tomato purée and capers. Bring to the boil, then cover and simmer for 15 minutes.

Meanwhile, cook the spaghetti in boiling salted water till tender. Drain thoroughly. Return to the pan and add the tomato and anchovy sauce and the black olives. Stir over a low heat for 3 minutes. Adjust seasoning to taste and serve hot.

Prawn pilaf

Overall timing 1 hour

Freezing Not suitable

To serve 4

2	Large onions	2
2	Fresh green chillies	2
2	Garlic cloves	2
8 oz	Streaky bacon rashers	225 g
1 tbsp	Oil	15 ml
8 oz	Long-grain rice	225 g
14 oz	Can of tomatoes	397 g
	Salt	
$\frac{3}{4}$ pint	Chicken stock	400 ml
1 lb	Shelled prawns	450 g
2 tbsp	Chopped parsley	2x15 ml
2 tbsp	Grated Parmesan cheese	2x15 ml

Peel and slice onions. Deseed and slice chillies. Peel and crush garlic. Derind and chop bacon.

Heat the oil in a flameproof casserole. Add bacon and fry until well browned. Add the onions, chillies and garlic to the casserole. Cook until onions are soft and transparent but not brown, stirring occasionally.

Add the rice and stir for 2–3 minutes until grains are coated with oil. Add the tomatoes with their juice, salt and chicken stock. Bring rapidly to the boil, then reduce heat, cover and simmer for 15 minutes on a very low heat.

Stir and add the prawns. Cover and cook for a further 5 minutes.

Turn mixture into warmed serving dish. Sprinkle with parsley and cheese and serve immediately.

Arabian pilaf

Overall timing 30 minutes

Freezing Not suitable

To serve 4

1 oz	Butter	25 g
2 oz	Capelli d'angelo (angels' hair pasta)	50 g
$1\frac{1}{4}$ pints	Chicken stock	700 ml
8 oz	Long grain rice	225 g
2 tbsp	Grated Parmesan cheese	2x15 ml
	Salt and pepper	

Melt the butter in a saucepan. Break up the pasta, add to the pan and fry, stirring, over a moderate heat till golden. Remove from pan and reserve.

Add the stock to the pan and bring to the boil. Stir in the rice, bring back to the boil and simmer gently for 15 minutes till the rice is just tender.

Stir in the fried pasta and cook for 2–3 minutes till pasta and rice are tender and all the liquid has been absorbed. Stir in Parmesan and seasoning with a fork. Transfer to a warmed serving dish and serve immediately.

Pizza succulenta

Overall timing 1 hour 10 minutes

Freezing Suitable: reheat in 400°F (200°C) Gas 6 oven for 30–40 minutes

To serve 6

5 oz	Strong plain flour	150 g
	Salt and pepper	
$1\frac{1}{2}$ teasp	Dried yeast	7.5 ml
$\frac{1}{2}$ teasp	Sugar	2.5 ml
5 tbsp	Lukewarm water	5x15 ml
3 tbsp	Oil	3x15 ml
4 oz	Mushrooms	125 g
1	Garlic clove	1
14 oz	Can of tomatoes	397 g
1 teasp	Dried oregano	5 ml
4 oz	Cooked ham	125 g
6 oz	Mozzarella cheese	175 g
1	Can of anchovy fillets	1

To make the base, sift flour and $\frac{1}{2}$ teasp (2.5 ml) salt into a large bowl. Place yeast in a small bowl and add sugar and warm water. Cover and leave in a warm place for 10 minutes or until frothy.

Make a well in the flour, add the yeast mixture and mix to a soft dough. Cover with a damp cloth and leave in warm place for 30 minutes.

To make topping, heat 2 tbsp (2x15 ml) of the oil in a saucepan. Slice mushrooms and fry gently for 3 minutes. Peel and crush garlic and add to pan with drained tomatoes, oregano and seasoning.

Preheat the oven to 475°F (240°C) Gas 9.

Knead the dough gently on a floured surface, roll out and line greased 11 inch (28 cm) pizza pan. Cover with tomato mixture. Finely chop the ham and scatter over. Slice cheese and arrange on top with drained anchovies. Sprinkle with remaining oil and bake for 20 minutes.

Gnocchi

Overall timing 50 minutes plus cooling

Freezing Suitable: bake from frozen, allowing 1 hour

To serve 4

1½ pints	Milk	850ml
6oz	Coarse semolina	175g
	Salt and pepper	
	Grated nutmeg	
6oz	Grated Parmesan cheese	175g
1	Egg yolk	1
2 tbsp	Milk	2x15ml

Heat milk just to boiling in a saucepan, then sprinkle on semolina. Season with salt, pepper and nutmeg. Cook gently, stirring, for 4–5 minutes till mixture becomes solid. Remove pan from heat and beat in 4oz (125g) of the cheese. Pour into a greased Swiss roll tin. Leave in a cool place (not the refrigerator) for 45 minutes to 1 hour till cold.

Preheat the oven to 400°F (200°C) Gas 6.

Cut the cooled mixture into about 20 rounds, 2½ inches (6.5cm) in diameter. Arrange the rounds, overlapping them, in a greased round ovenproof dish. Beat egg yolk and milk and pour over. Sprinkle with the rest of the cheese and bake for 30 minutes till golden brown. Serve immediately.

Three-cheese savouries

Overall timing 10 minutes plus chilling

Freezing Not suitable

To serve 6

4oz	Danish blue cheese	125g
3	Petits suisses cheeses	3
4oz	Gruyère cheese	125g
2 tbsp	Chopped fresh herbs	2x15ml
4oz	Dried breadcrumbs	125g

Mash Danish blue and Petits suisses cheeses together in a bowl with a fork. Grate Gruyère and add to bowl with herbs. Mix well together.

Shape into flat cakes or cylinders and coat in breadcrumbs. Place on a plate and chill for 3 hours before serving with toast, crisp biscuits or French bread.

Variation

Use a mixture of cream, cottage and curd cheeses, and flavour with 2 cloves of crushed garlic creamed with salt. Make into shapes (use biscuit or scone cutters) and coat in breadcrumbs or finely chopped parsley. Or use prepared pepper for steak which is a combination of pepper and mustard. Chill as above before serving.

Cheesy tapioca fritters

Overall timing 1 hour

Freezing Not suitable

To serve 6

1	Medium-size onion	1
4oz	Flaked tapioca	125g
1½ pints	Milk	850ml
1	Bay leaf	1
	Salt and pepper	
3	Eggs	3
6oz	Cheese	175g
½ teasp	Powdered mustard	2.5ml
	Oil for deep frying	
	Sprigs of parsley	

Peel and finely chop the onion. Put into a saucepan with the tapioca, milk and bay leaf. Season and bring to the boil, stirring. Cook for about 30 minutes, stirring occasionally, till thick and creamy. Remove from the heat.

Separate the eggs and beat the yolks one at a time into the mixture. Grate the cheese and add to the mixture with mustard. Mix well and leave to cool.

Heat oil in a deep-fryer to 340°F (170°C).

Whisk the egg whites till stiff but not dry, then fold into the tapioca mixture with a metal spoon. Drop a few large spoonfuls of the mixture into the oil and fry for 3–4 minutes till crisp and golden. Drain on kitchen paper. Sprinkle with salt and serve hot, garnished with parsley.

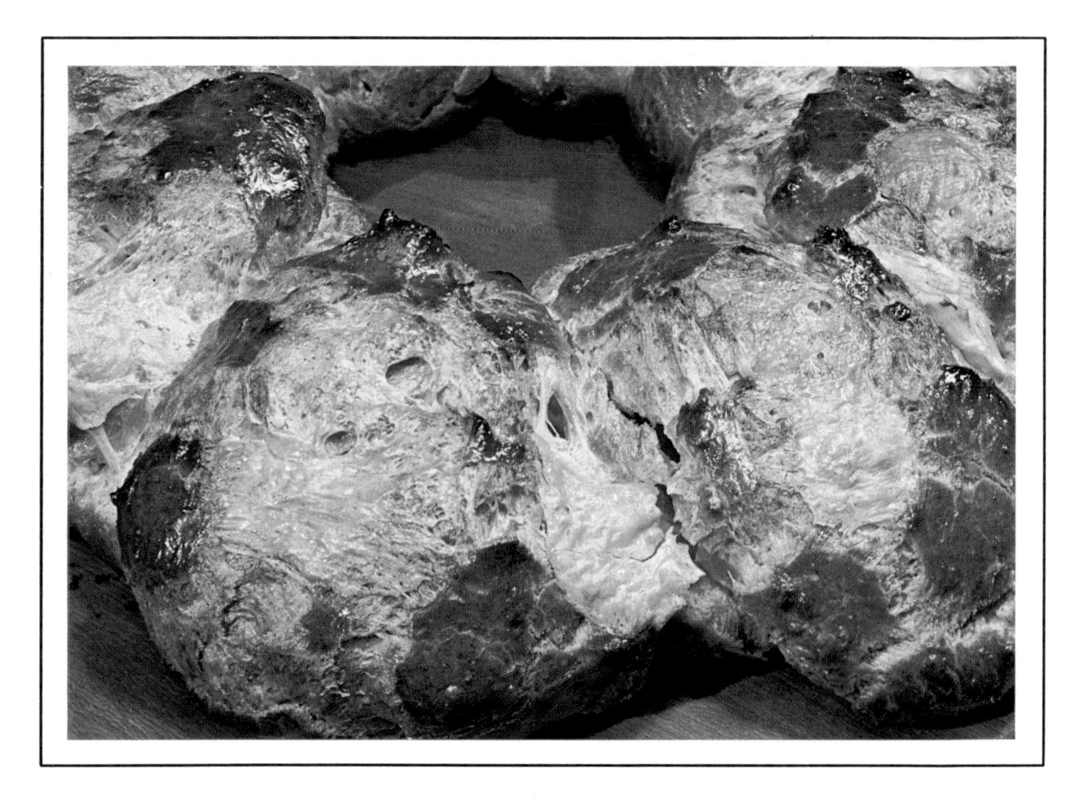

Gougère

Overall timing $1\frac{1}{2}$ hours

Freezing Not suitable

To serve 6

7 fl oz	Water	200 ml
$\frac{1}{2}$ teasp	Salt	2.5 ml
4 oz	Butter	125 g
$3\frac{1}{2}$ oz	Plain flour	100 g
4	Eggs	4
8 oz	Gruyère cheese	225 g

Preheat oven to 400°F (200°C) Gas 6.

Put water and salt into a saucepan, with 3 oz (75 g) of the butter, chopped. Bring to the boil, stirring to melt the butter. Remove from heat and quickly add the flour all at once, stirring well. Return pan to heat and beat till the paste is smooth and leaves the sides of the pan cleanly. Remove from heat and allow to cool slightly.

Add three of the eggs, one at a time, beating well between additions. Grate 5 oz (150 g) of the cheese and stir into the paste.

With a large spoon, make a ring of the paste on a greased baking tray. Beat the remaining egg and brush over paste. Dice remaining cheese and place on top of the paste with tiny pieces of the remaining butter.

Bake for 20 minutes, then lower heat to 375°F (190°C) Gas 5, and bake for a further 20–25 minutes. Serve hot.

Sauerkraut cheese rolls

Overall timing $1\frac{1}{2}$ hours

Freezing Not suitable

To serve 6

8 oz	Plain flour	225 g
	Salt	
8 oz	Cream cheese	225 g
5 oz	Butter	150 g
2	Eggs	2
$\frac{1}{4}$ pint	Carton of soured cream	150 ml
	Grated nutmeg	
1	Small onion	1
3 oz	Cheese	75 g
Filling		
4 oz	Streaky bacon	125 g
1 lb	Can of sauerkraut	454 g
1 tbsp	Sugar	15 ml
	Salt and pepper	
1	Bay leaf	1

Sift flour and salt into bowl and rub in cream cheese and 4 oz (125 g) butter. Knead till smooth, then chill for 30 minutes.

Meanwhile, for the filling, derind and chop bacon. Place in saucepan and cook till golden, then add sauerkraut, sugar, seasoning and bay leaf. Cover and cook gently for 30 minutes. Remove bay leaf. Cool.

Preheat oven to 400°F (200°C) Gas 6.

Roll out dough to rectangle 18x10 inches (45x25 cm). Spoon filling over dough, leaving border. Beginning at long edge, roll up, then cut roll into six smaller rolls. Arrange rolls in greased ovenproof dish.

Beat eggs with soured cream, salt and nutmeg. Pour over the rolls. Peel and slice onion. Grate cheese. Top rolls with onion rings, cheese and remaining butter. Bake for 40 minutes.

Pastry and egg dishes

Puffed potato pie

Overall timing $1\frac{3}{4}$ hours

Freezing Not suitable

To serve 8

$1\frac{1}{2}$ lb	Frozen puff pastry	700g
$2\frac{1}{2}$ lb	New or small waxy potatoes	1.1kg
	Salt and pepper	
1	Large onion	1
2 tbsp	Chopped parsley	2x15ml
$\frac{1}{4}$ pint	Carton of double cream	150ml
1	Egg	1

Thaw pastry. Preheat oven to 425°F (220°C) Gas 7.

Roll out two-thirds of dough and use to line a 9 inch (23cm) springform tin, leaving excess overhanging the edges. Chill.

Scrape or peel the potatoes and slice thinly (use a mandolin for best results). Blanch in boiling salted water for 2 minutes. Drain thoroughly. Peel and finely chop the onion.

Arrange potato slices, onion and parsley in neat layers in the pastry case, seasoning well. Pour the cream over. Roll out the remaining dough to make a lid and cut a small hole in the centre. Seal the edges with beaten egg. Decorate with dough trimmings. Make a foil chimney and put it in the central hole.

Brush the top of the pie carefully with beaten egg. Bake for 20 minutes. Reduce the temperature to 350°F (180°C) Gas 4 and bake for a further 30 minutes till well risen and golden brown. Remove from the tin and serve hot.

Tomato flan

Overall timing 1 hour plus chilling

Freezing Suitable: reheat in 350°F (180°C) Gas 4 oven for 25–30 minutes

To serve 6

9 oz	**Plain flour**	250 g
	Salt	
4 tbsp	**Soured cream**	4x15 ml
5 oz	**Butter**	150 g
Filling		
5	**Tomatoes**	5
6 oz	**Cheese**	175 g
8	**Thin slices of French bread**	8
¼ pint	**Carton of double cream**	150 ml
¼ pint	**Carton of soured cream**	141 g
4	**Eggs**	4
	Salt	
	Grated nutmeg	
½ teasp	**Paprika**	2.5 ml
1 oz	**Butter**	25 g

Sift flour and salt into bowl. Add soured cream, dot with butter pieces and knead lightly until smooth. Chill for 30 minutes.

Thinly slice tomatoes. Slice cheese and cut crusts off bread.

Preheat oven to 400°F (200°C) Gas 6.

Roll out dough and use to line 12 inch (30 cm) flan tin. Cover with layer of sliced tomatoes, then cheese and bread.

Beat double cream with soured cream, eggs, a pinch each of salt and nutmeg, and paprika. Pour into flan tin and dot top with butter. Bake for 30–40 minutes until firm and golden. Serve hot.

Onion quiche

Overall timing $1\frac{1}{2}$ hours

Freezing Suitable: reheat from frozen, covered, in 350°F (180°C) Gas 4 oven for 20 minutes

To serve 4

1 lb	Medium-size onions	450 g
2 oz	Lard	50 g
4 oz	Smoked streaky bacon	125 g
6 oz	Rich shortcrust pastry	175 g
3	Eggs	3
$\frac{1}{4}$ pint	Milk	150 ml
$\frac{1}{4}$ pint	Carton of single cream	150 ml
	Salt and pepper	

Preheat the oven to 400°F (200°C) Gas 6.

Peel and thinly slice the onions. Melt the lard in a frying pan and fry the onions over a moderate heat till pale golden.

Derind and dice the bacon and add to the pan. Fry for a further 4–5 minutes till the onions and bacon are golden brown.

Roll out the dough and use to line an $8\frac{1}{2}$ inch (22 cm) flan dish. Prick the bottom and bake blind for 15 minutes.

Remove foil and baking beans and spread the onion and bacon mixture over the pastry base. Mix the eggs with the milk and cream and season to taste. Pour over the onions.

Bake for a further 25 minutes till lightly set and golden. Serve hot with mixed salads.

Welsh parsley flan

Overall timing 1 hour

Freezing Suitable: reheat from frozen in 350°F (180°C) Gas 4 oven for 25 minutes

To serve 4–6

8 oz	Shortcrust pastry	225 g
4 oz	Streaky bacon	125 g
1 oz	Butter	25 g
3	Eggs	3
½ pint	Milk	300 ml
3 tbsp	Chopped parsley	3x15 ml
	Salt and pepper	

Preheat the oven to 400°F (200°C) Gas 6.

Roll out the dough and use to line a 9 inch (23 cm) flan tin. Prick the bottom with a fork and bake blind for 15 minutes.

Meanwhile, derind and chop the bacon. Melt the butter in a frying pan and fry the bacon till golden. Arrange the bacon in the flan case. Reduce oven temperature to 350°F (180°C) Gas 4.

Beat the eggs, milk and parsley together, season to taste and pour over the bacon. Bake for a further 20–25 minutes till set. Serve hot or cold.

Sicilian fish pie

Overall timing 2 hours

Freezing Not suitable

To serve 8

12oz	Rich shortcrust pastry	350g
2 tbsp	Caster sugar	2x15ml
½ teasp	Grated lemon rind	2.5ml
12oz	White fish steaks	350g
1	Large stalk of celery	1
3oz	Stoned green olives	75g
1	Large onion	1
3 tbsp	Olive oil	3x15ml
1 tbsp	Drained capers	15ml
2 tbsp	Tomato purée	2x15ml
	Salt and pepper	
3	Courgettes	3
1	Egg	1
3 tbsp	Plain flour	3x15ml
	Oil for deep frying	
1	Egg yolk	1

Make pastry, adding sugar and lemon rind with 3 egg yolks. Cube fish; chop celery; slice olives. Peel and thinly slice onion. Heat oil in a saucepan, add onion and fry till golden. Add celery, olives, capers, tomato purée, fish, ¼ pint (150ml) water and seasoning. Simmer for 15 minutes.

Preheat oven to 350°F (180°C) Gas 4.

Cut courgettes into thin fingers. Beat egg; season flour. Dip courgettes into egg, then into flour. Deep fry till golden. Drain.

Divide dough into thirds. Roll out one and use to line a greased and floured 8 inch (20cm) springform tin. Roll out remaining dough to two 8 inch (20cm) rounds.

Layer fish mixture, courgettes and dough rounds in tin. Brush with beaten egg yolk and bake for 50 minutes. Remove from tin and serve hot.

Cheese flan

Overall timing 1½ hours

Freezing Suitable: reheat in 425°F (220°C) Gas 7 oven for 10–15 minutes

To serve 4–6

5 oz	Butter	150 g
¼ pint	Water	150 ml
	Salt and pepper	
8 oz	Self-raising flour	225 g
2	Medium-size onions	2
1 tbsp	Plain flour	15 ml
4 fl oz	Milk	120 ml
3	Eggs	3
¼ teasp	Grated nutmeg	1.25 ml
	Cayenne pepper	
4 oz	Cheddar cheese	125 g
4 oz	Gruyère cheese	125 g

Melt 4 oz (125 g) of the butter. Cool slightly, then stir in 3 tbsp (3x15 ml) of the water and salt. Sift self-raising flour into a bowl. Slowly add butter mixture and mix until smooth. Chill for 30 minutes.

Preheat the oven to 350°F (180°C) Gas 4.

Peel and chop onions. Melt remaining butter in a saucepan and fry onions for 10 minutes until soft. Cool.

Mix plain flour and a little of the milk in a bowl, then add the rest of the milk and the remaining water. Separate the eggs. Mix the yolks into the flour and milk mixture. Season with salt, pepper, nutmeg and a pinch of cayenne. Beat egg whites till stiff, then fold into yolk mixture.

Roll out dough and use to line a greased 9 inch (23 cm) flan tin. Spread onions over bottom of flan, then grate both sorts of cheese on top. Cover with egg and milk mixture.

Bake for 15 minutes. Reduce heat to 325°F (170°C) Gas 3 and bake for a further 45 minutes. Serve hot.

Rich leek flan

Overall timing 1 hour

Freezing Suitable: reheat from frozen, covered, in 375°F (190°C) Gas 5 oven for 35 minutes

To serve 6–8

13oz	Frozen puff pastry	375g
2lb	Leeks	900g
2oz	Butter	50g
1 tbsp	Plain flour	15ml
$\frac{1}{2}$ pint	Light stock	300ml
	Salt and pepper	
1	Egg	1
1	Egg yolk	1
$\frac{1}{2}$ pint	Carton of single cream	284ml

Thaw pastry. Preheat the oven to 425°F (220°C) Gas 7.

Trim leeks. Cut into 1 inch (2.5cm) lengths. Blanch in boiling water for 5 minutes, then drain thoroughly.

Melt butter in a frying pan and fry the leeks for 5 minutes. Sprinkle with flour and cook until lightly browned. Gradually stir in the stock and bring to the boil. Season and cook gently for 10 minutes.

Meanwhile, roll out dough and use to line a 9 inch (23cm) flan dish. Prick bottom several times with a fork.

Beat the whole egg, yolk and cream together in a bowl. Remove leeks from heat and add cream mixture. Pour into flan dish and spread evenly. Bake for 30 minutes till lightly set and golden. Serve hot.

Crusty mushroom bread

Overall timing 1 hour

Freezing Suitable: cook after thawing

To serve 6–8

1	**Round loaf of bread**	1
4oz	**Butter**	125g
1lb	**Mushrooms**	450g
	Salt and pepper	
3 tbsp	**Lemon juice**	3x15ml
½ pint	**White sauce**	300ml
2	**Eggs**	2

Preheat the oven to 350°F (180°C) Gas 4.

Slice the top off the bread and scoop out most of the crumbs, leaving a ½ inch (12.5mm) thick shell. Spread the inside with half the butter, place on a baking tray and bake for 10 minutes.

Meanwhile, finely chop the mushrooms. Melt the remaining butter in a saucepan and fry the mushrooms for 5 minutes, stirring frequently. Add salt, pepper and lemon juice. Stir the mushrooms into the white sauce.

Separate the eggs and beat the egg yolks, one at a time, into the sauce. Return to the heat and heat through gently. Whisk the egg whites till stiff but not dry. Gently fold into the mushroom mixture.

Pour the mixture into the bread shell and sprinkle the top with a few of the scooped out breadcrumbs, grated. Bake for 30 minutes till well risen and crisp. Serve hot.

Spinach flan

Overall timing 50 minutes

Freezing Not suitable

To serve 6

12 oz	Wholemeal shortcrust pastry	350 g
2 lb	Spinach	900 g
	Salt and pepper	
½ teasp	Grated nutmeg	2.5 ml
	Bunch of marjoram	
4 oz	Streaky bacon	125 g
3 oz	Butter	75 g
1	Onion	1
1 oz	Sultanas	25 g
4 tbsp	Single cream	4x15 ml
6 oz	Mozzarella cheese	175 g

Preheat the oven to 400°F (200°C) Gas 6.

Roll out dough and line 9 inch (23 cm) flan tin. Bake blind for 30 minutes.

Meanwhile, cook spinach with salt and nutmeg for 10 minutes. Drain and chop. Chop marjoram and add to spinach.

Derind and chop bacon. Melt half butter in a frying pan and fry bacon till crisp. Scatter bacon over base of flan.

Add remaining butter to pan. Peel and finely chop onion and fry till transparent. Add spinach mixture, three-quarters of sultanas, cream and seasoning. Cook for 5 minutes. Spread in flan case.

Slice cheese and arrange on top. Sprinkle with rest of sultanas and bake for 10 minutes.

Prawn scrambled eggs

Overall timing 15 minutes

Freezing Not suitable

To serve 4

2 oz	Butter	50 g
8 oz	Shelled prawns	225 g
8	Large eggs	8
	Salt and pepper	

Melt half the butter in a saucepan, add prawns and fry gently for 3–4 minutes.

Break the eggs into a bowl, add seasoning and beat lightly with a fork. Pour on to the prawns and stir gently but evenly till the eggs are lightly set.

Remove from the heat, quickly stir in the remaining butter and season to taste. Divide between warmed serving dishes and serve immediately with hot toast.

Roe and egg toasts

Overall timing 30 minutes

Freezing Not suitable

To serve 6		
12oz	Soft herring roes	350g
	Salt and pepper	
3oz	Butter	75g
2 tbsp	Plain flour	2x15ml
½ pint	Milk	300ml
2	Anchovy fillets	2
3	Hard-boiled eggs	3
1 tbsp	Lemon juice	15ml
6	Slices of bread	6
6oz	Smoked cod's roe	175g

Poach soft roes in boiling salted water for 5 minutes. Drain and chop.

Melt 2oz (50g) of the butter in a saucepan, stir in the flour and cook for 1 minute. Gradually add the milk and bring to the boil, stirring.

Pound the anchovy fillets in a bowl. Shell the eggs and cut in half. Sieve the yolks and stir into the sauce with the anchovies, soft roes, lemon juice and seasoning. Heat through.

Preheat the grill. Toast the bread, spread with remaining butter and arrange on the grill pan. Spread the soft roe mixture over. Finely chop the egg whites and use to decorate the toast. Cut the smoked cod's roe into 12 thin slices and place two on each piece of toast. Grill for 2–3 minutes till bubbling and golden. Serve hot.

Egg and ham moulds

Overall timing 20 minutes

Freezing Not suitable

To serve 4		
2oz	Softened butter	50g
6oz	Cooked ham	175g
8	Eggs	8
	Salt	
1	Tomato	1

Grease 8 dariole moulds with the butter. Finely chop the ham and press onto the bottoms and sides of the moulds. Carefully break an egg into each mould and sprinkle with salt.

Put moulds into heatproof dish containing a little boiling water, cover and cook for 8–10 minutes till eggs are lightly set.

Run a knife blade around the inside of each mould and invert on to a warmed serving plate. Garnish with tomato slices and serve with a green salad.

Egg and parsley mayonnaise

Overall timing 15 minutes plus chilling

Freezing Not suitable

To serve 4

8	Hard-boiled eggs	8
2	Spring onions	2
3 tbsp	Chopped parsley	3x15 ml
$\frac{1}{4}$ pint	Thick mayonnaise	150 ml
$\frac{1}{4}$ pint	Carton of soured cream	150 ml
	Salt and pepper	

Shell and slice the hard-boiled eggs. Trim the spring onions and slice thinly. Arrange half the eggs in a shallow dish and sprinkle the spring onions and 2 tbsp (2x15 ml) of the parsley over.

Mix together the mayonnaise and soured cream and add seasoning to taste. Spoon three-quarters of the mayonnaise mixture over the eggs. Arrange the remaining egg slices decoratively on top and spoon the rest of the mayonnaise between them.

Chill for 1 hour before serving. Sprinkle with the reserved parsley and serve with slices of crusty brown bread.

Eggs with sausages

Overall timing 15 minutes

Freezing Not suitable

To serve 2–4		
1 tbsp	Oil	15 ml
12	Chipolatas	12
1 oz	Butter	25 g
4	Eggs	4
3 tbsp	Tomato ketchup	3x15 ml
	Pepper	

Heat the oil in a frying pan. Cook the chipolatas till golden all over, then remove from the pan.

Melt butter in the pan, break in the eggs and place chipolatas over whites. Fry for 2–3 minutes, then spoon ketchup around the edge of the pan. Sprinkle with pepper and serve with toast and grilled tomatoes.

Variation

Sprinkle grated cheese over the eggs and chipolatas and grill until the cheese has melted and is golden brown.

Deep-fried eggs

Overall timing 15 minutes

Freezing Not suitable

To serve 4

	Oil for frying	
8	Eggs	8
	Salt and pepper	
2	Tomatoes	2
	Sprigs of parsley	

Half-fill a shallow frying pan with oil and heat to 370°F (188°C) or until a cube of bread browns in 1 minute. Swirl fat round with a spoon. Break an egg into a cup and carefully slide into the hot oil. Cook for 1–2 minutes, basting with the hot oil all the time and turning the egg once or twice.

Remove from pan with a draining spoon and drain on kitchen paper. Sprinkle with salt and pepper. Keep hot while you fry remaining eggs in the same way. Garnish with tomato wedges and parsley sprigs and serve hot with toast.

Chervil omelette

Overall timing 15 minutes

Freezing Not suitable

To serve 4

8	Eggs	8
	Salt and pepper	
3 tbsp	Chopped fresh chervil	3x15 ml
1 tbsp	Chopped parsley	15 ml
2 oz	Butter	50 g

Break the eggs into a bowl. Season with salt and pepper, add herbs and beat together lightly.

Melt one-quarter of the butter in an omelette pan over a high heat. When the butter begins to froth, pour in a quarter of the egg mixture. As the omelette starts to set, run a spatula round the edge to loosen it and tilt pan to let uncooked egg run underneath. When firm at the edges but still runny in the centre, fold omelette over and slide on to a warmed serving plate. Keep it hot while you make three more omelettes in the same way. Serve with a tomato salad.

Noodle tortilla

Overall timing 45 minutes

Freezing Not suitable

To serve 4

12oz	Noodles	350g
	Salt	
3oz	Butter	75g
4oz	Cottage cheese	125g
3	Eggs	3
$\frac{1}{4}$ teasp	Ground allspice	1.25ml
2 tbsp	Chopped parsley	2x15ml

Cook the noodles in boiling salted water for about 5 minutes till tender. Drain thoroughly and put into a warm bowl. Stir in 2oz (50g) of the butter and the sieved cottage cheese. Lightly beat the eggs and stir into the noodles with salt, allspice and chopped parsley.

Preheat the grill. Melt the remaining butter in a frying pan. Add the noodle mixture and smooth the top. Cook over a moderate heat for 5 minutes till lightly set. Put the pan under the grill to brown the top.

Turn omelette on to a warmed serving plate and serve immediately.

Italian shredded omelette

Overall timing 35 minutes

Freezing Not suitable

To serve 4

1	Small onion	1
1	Garlic clove	1
1	Stalk of celery	1
1	Carrot	1
2oz	Streaky bacon rashers	50g
1 tbsp	Oil	15ml
14oz	Can of tomatoes	397g
	Salt and pepper	
9	Eggs	9
1 teasp	Chopped fresh mint	5ml
3 tbsp	Chopped parsley	3x15ml
2oz	Butter	50g

Peel and finely chop the onion. Peel and crush the garlic. Trim and chop the celery. Scrape and thinly slice the carrot. Derind and finely chop the bacon.

Heat the oil in a saucepan, add the bacon and vegetables and fry gently for 5 minutes. Add the tomatoes and juice, garlic and seasoning, bring to the boil and simmer for 20 minutes, stirring to break up the tomatoes.

Meanwhile, lightly beat the eggs in a bowl with the mint, parsley and seasoning. Melt one-third of the butter in a frying pan. Add one-third of the egg mixture and cook over a moderate heat, drawing the liquid into the centre as the mixture begins to set. When set, slide the omelette on to a board. Make two more omelettes in the same way.

Roll the omelettes loosely and cut into strips about ½ inch (12.5mm) wide. Add to the tomato sauce and heat through for 3 minutes. Season to taste and pour into a warmed serving dish.

Baked eggs in potatoes

Overall timing 2 hours

Freezing Not suitable

To serve 4

4x10 oz	Potatoes	4x275 g
2 oz	Butter	50 g
	Salt and pepper	
2 oz	Cheese	50 g
4	Small eggs	4
4 tbsp	Double cream	4x15 ml
2 teasp	Chopped chives	2x5 ml

Preheat the oven to 400°F (200°C) Gas 6.

Scrub and dry the potatoes and push a metal skewer lengthways through each one. Place on a baking tray and rub a little of the butter over the skins. Bake for 1–1¼ hours.

Remove from the oven. Increase the temperature to 450°F (230°C) Gas 8.

Cut a slice lengthways off each potato and scoop out the insides, leaving a shell about ½ inch (12.5 mm) thick. Mash the scooped-out potato (plus any from the lids) in a bowl with the remaining butter and seasoning. Grate cheese and beat into potato mixture.

Press the mixture back into the potato shells, leaving a hollow in the centre large enough for an egg. Place on baking tray. Carefully break an egg into each potato. Season and spoon the cream over. Return to the oven and bake for 8–10 minutes till the eggs are lightly set. Sprinkle the chives over and serve hot.

Egg and pea scramble

Overall timing 50 minutes

Freezing Not suitable

To serve 2–4

2lb	Fresh peas	900g
1	Onion	1
2oz	Streaky bacon rashers	50g
2oz	Butter	50g
	Salt and pepper	
2oz	Cheese	50g
4	Eggs	4
2oz	Fresh breadcrumbs	50g

Shell peas. Peel and thinly slice the onion; derind and dice the bacon. Melt the butter in a saucepan and gently fry the onion and bacon till transparent.

Add the peas and salt and enough water to half cover them. Bring to the boil, then cover and simmer for 15–20 minutes till the peas are tender and most of the liquid has evaporated.

Grate cheese. Lightly beat the eggs in a bowl with the breadcrumbs and pepper. Pour over the peas and cook, stirring gently, till the eggs are lightly set. Serve immediately.

Chicken liver pancakes

Overall timing 45 minutes

Freezing Suitable: add cream and cheese and bake from frozen, covered, allowing 30–40 minutes

To serve 4

4 oz	Chicken livers	125 g
8 oz	Button mushrooms	225 g
1	Small onion	1
2 oz	Butter	50 g
	Salt and pepper	
6	Slices of cooked ham	6
3 tbsp	Single cream	3x15 ml
	Grated nutmeg	
2 oz	Cheddar cheese	50 g
Pancakes		
5 oz	Plain flour	150 g
¼ teasp	Salt	1.25 ml
2	Eggs	2
½ pint	Beer	300 ml
	Oil for frying	

Chop chicken livers. Chop mushrooms. Peel and finely chop onion. Melt butter in a saucepan and gently fry mushrooms and onion for 5 minutes. Add chopped livers and fry for 3–4 minutes. Season with salt and pepper.

To make pancakes, sift flour and salt into a bowl and make a well in the centre. Add eggs and beer and beat to a smooth batter. Heat a little oil in an 8 inch (20 cm) pancake or frying pan and make 12 pancakes.

Preheat oven to 400°F (200°C) Gas 6.

Cut slices of ham in half. Place one half on each pancake. Divide liver mixture between pancakes, then roll them up. Place side by side in greased baking dish. Pour cream over and sprinkle with nutmeg and grated cheese.

Bake for 15–20 minutes, or grill for 5 minutes. Serve hot.

Chive and mushroom pancakes

Overall timing 1¼ hours

Freezing Suitable: bake filled pancakes with sauce in 350°F (180°C) Gas 4 oven for 20 minutes

To serve 4–6

1 lb	Button mushrooms	450 g
1 oz	Butter	25 g
½ pint	Milk	300 ml
	Salt and pepper	
¼ teasp	Grated nutmeg	1.25 ml
1½ tbsp	Lemon juice	22.5 ml
½ pint	White sauce	300 ml
Pancakes		
5 oz	Plain flour	150 g
¼ teasp	Salt	1.25 ml
2	Eggs	2
2 tbsp	Chopped chives	2x15 ml
	Oil for frying	

Finely chop mushrooms. Melt butter in a saucepan and fry mushrooms for 3 minutes. Add milk, seasoning, nutmeg and lemon juice. Bring to the boil and simmer for 10 minutes. Strain, reserving the milk for the pancakes.

Make the pancakes as left, using the reserved milk instead of beer and adding the chives to the batter. Fry 12 pancakes.

Preheat the oven to 350°F (180°C) Gas 4.

Divide the mushroom filling between the pancakes and roll them to enclose the filling. Arrange in a greased ovenproof dish and pour the white sauce over. Bake for about 20 minutes. Serve immediately, garnished with extra fluted mushrooms, if liked.

Vegetable dishes

Spinach ring

Overall timing 1 hour 20 minutes

Freezing Not suitable

To serve 4–6

2lb	Spinach	900g
2oz	Butter	50g
4 tbsp	Plain flour	4x15ml
½ pint	Milk	300ml
2 tbsp	Grated Parmesan cheese	2x15ml
	Salt and pepper	
3	Eggs	3
	Tomato sauce (see page 19)	

Preheat the oven to 375°F (190°C) Gas 5.

Wash and pick over the spinach and put into a saucepan with only the water that clings to it. Cover and cook for 5 minutes. Drain thoroughly and purée in a blender or a food mill.

Melt the butter in a saucepan, add the flour and cook for 1 minute. Gradually add the milk and bring to the boil, stirring constantly, to make a thick sauce. Simmer for 2 minutes, then remove from the heat and beat in the spinach, cheese and seasoning.

Separate the eggs. Beat the yolks into the spinach mixture. Whisk the whites till stiff but not dry and fold carefully into the spinach. Spoon the mixture into a greased 3 pint (1.7 litre) ring mould and smooth top. Bake for about 35 minutes till well risen and lightly set.

Run a knife around the edge of the mould and turn the spinach ring out on to a warmed serving dish. Spoon the hot tomato sauce over and serve immediately.

Vegetable moussaka

Overall timing 2 hours

Freezing Not suitable

To serve 4–6

2	Large onions	2
1	Garlic clove	1
1	Large aubergine	1
	Salt and pepper	
2oz	Butter	50g
4oz	Continental lentils	125g
2 tbsp	Tomato purée	2x15ml
1 pint	Light stock	560ml
4	Small globe artichokes	4
1 tbsp	Lemon juice	15ml
	Bouquet garni	
4 tbsp	Oil	4x15ml
	Sprigs of parsley	

Peel and finely chop onions; peel and crush garlic. Slice aubergine, sprinkle with salt and leave to drain for 15 minutes.

Melt the butter in a saucepan, add onion and garlic and fry till golden. Add lentils, tomato purée and stock and simmer for about 1 hour till a thick purée.

Meanwhile, remove stem and coarse outer leaves from artichokes. Bring a pan of water to the boil, add lemon juice, bouquet garni and artichokes and simmer for 20–30 minutes till tender.

Rinse aubergines and dry on kitchen paper. Heat oil in a frying pan, add aubergines and fry till crisp and golden.

Preheat oven to 350°F (180°C) Gas 4.

Drain artichokes thoroughly, cut in half and remove chokes. Arrange cut sides up in greased ovenproof dish. Pour half lentil mixture over artichokes, then cover with half fried aubergine slices. Repeat the layers of lentil and aubergine and press down lightly. Bake for 30 minutes. Turn out and serve hot, garnished with parsley.

Courgettes baked with cheese

Overall timing 1 hour

Freezing Not suitable

To serve 4

$1\frac{3}{4}$ lb	Courgettes	750g
	Oil for frying	
	Tomato sauce (see page 19)	
4 tbsp	Grated Parmesan cheese	4x15 ml
$\frac{1}{2}$ teasp	Dried basil	2.5 ml
5 oz	Mozzarella cheese	150g
	Salt and pepper	
1 oz	Butter	25g

Trim courgettes, then thickly slice them lengthways. Heat oil in a large frying pan. When oil is very hot, add courgettes – in two batches if necessary – and cook till golden on both sides. Remove from pan with draining spoon and drain on kitchen paper.

Preheat oven to 400°F (200°C) Gas 6.

Layer courgettes, tomato sauce, Parmesan, basil and slices of Mozzarella in a greased ovenproof dish, seasoning each layer well. Continue till all the ingredients are used up. Dot with butter. Bake till the cheese is melted and lightly golden on top.

Boxty on the griddle

Overall timing 40 minutes

Freezing Suitable: reheat from frozen in 400°F (200°C) Gas 6 oven for 10 minutes

To serve 4

8oz	Waxy potatoes	225g
4oz	Cooked mashed potatoes	125g
4oz	Plain flour	125g
$\frac{1}{2}$ teasp	Bicarbonate of soda	2.5ml
$\frac{3}{4}$ pint	Milk	400ml
	Salt and pepper	
	Oil for frying	

Peel the potatoes and grate into a large bowl. Add the mashed potatoes, sifted flour and bicarbonate of soda and mix together well. Make a well in the centre and gradually stir in enough milk to make a stiff batter. Season well.

Heat a lightly oiled griddle or heavy-based frying pan. Drop the batter in large spoonfuls on to the griddle or pan and cook over a moderate heat for 4 minutes on each side till crisp and golden.

Serve hot with fried black pudding, bacon and eggs.

Mushroom loaf

Overall timing 1 hour

Freezing Not suitable

To serve 4

$1\frac{1}{2}$ lb	Button mushrooms	700 g
$1\frac{1}{2}$ oz	Butter	40 g
$\frac{1}{2}$ pint	White sauce	300 ml
	Salt and pepper	
	Grated nutmeg	
3	Eggs	3

Preheat the oven to 350°F (180°C) Gas 4.

Trim the mushrooms. Reserve four for decoration and finely chop the rest. Melt 1 oz (25 g) butter in a saucepan and cook the chopped mushrooms for 5 minutes. Stir in the white sauce, then season with salt, pepper and a little grated nutmeg to taste.

Remove pan from heat and allow to cool slightly, then beat in the eggs one at a time. Pour the mixture into a greased 6 inch (15 cm) soufflé dish and bake for about 45 minutes till set.

Meanwhile, flute one of the reserved mushrooms and thinly slice the other three. Melt remaining butter in a saucepan and fry mushrooms till golden.

Turn out mushroom loaf and serve hot, garnished with fried mushrooms, on a bed of lettuce leaves.

Norwegian cauliflower

Overall timing 25 minutes

Freezing Not suitable

To serve 4

1	Cauliflower	1
	Salt and pepper	
1oz	Butter	25g
2oz	Fresh white breadcrumbs	50g
½ pint	Milk	300ml
	Pinch of sugar	
4oz	Shelled prawns	125g
1 tbsp	Brandy (optional)	15ml
3 tbsp	Single cream	3x15ml
	Sprigs of parsley	

Remove any leaves from the cauliflower and trim the stalk. Put cauliflower into a saucepan containing 1½ inches (4cm) of boiling salted water, cover and cook for 20 minutes.

Meanwhile, melt the butter in another pan, add breadcrumbs and milk and cook for a few minutes, stirring. Add salt, pepper and sugar. Set aside a few shelled prawns for the garnish and add the rest to the pan. Cook for 5 minutes more, stirring.

Remove pan from heat and add brandy, if used, and cream. Return to a gentle heat for 1 minute.

Drain cauliflower, place on a warmed serving dish and pour over sauce. Garnish with reserved prawns and parsley.

Stuffed baked potatoes

Overall timing $1\frac{1}{2}$ hours

Freezing Not suitable

To serve 8

8x8 oz	Waxy potatoes	8x225 g
1	Large onion	1
3 oz	Butter	75 g
8 oz	Cooked ham	225 g
6 tbsp	Dry white wine or cider	6x15 ml
2 oz	Fresh breadcrumbs	50 g
2 tbsp	Chopped parsley	2x15 ml
	Salt and pepper	
$\frac{1}{4}$ pint	Chicken stock	150 ml

Preheat the oven to 400°F (200°C) Gas 6.

Peel the potatoes. Cut a slice from one end of each so they stand upright. Cut a slice from the other end of each and hollow out the centres with a sharp knife, leaving a thick shell. Finely chop the scooped out pieces and slices cut from the tops of the potatoes.

Peel and finely chop the onion. Melt 1 oz (25 g) of the butter in a saucepan and fry the onion till transparent. Dice the ham and add to the pan with the wine or cider, chopped potatoes and breadcrumbs. Cover and cook for 5 minutes, then stir in the parsley and seasoning.

Spoon the mixture into the potatoes, pressing it down firmly. Stand potatoes upright in a greased ovenproof dish. Melt remaining butter with the stock and pour into the dish.

Bake for 50 minutes to 1 hour, basting frequently, till the potatoes are tender. Serve hot with a green salad.

Chicory rolls in cheese sauce

Overall timing $1\frac{1}{4}$ hours

Freezing Suitable: bake from frozen in cold oven set to 350°F (180°C) Gas 4 for 1 hour; increase to 450°F (230°C) Gas 8 for extra 10 minutes

To serve 4–6

4oz	Butter	125g
8	Large heads of chicory	8
2 tbsp	Lemon juice	2x15ml
1 teasp	Sugar	5ml
	Salt and pepper	
1oz	Plain flour	25g
$\frac{1}{2}$ pint	Milk	300ml
	Grated nutmeg	
2	Egg yolks	2
2oz	Grated Parmesan cheese	50g
8	Thin slices of cooked ham	8

Melt half butter in a saucepan and add chicory, lemon juice, sugar and seasoning. Cover and cook gently for about 30 minutes, turning the chicory occasionally.

Meanwhile, make the sauce. Melt 1oz (25g) of remaining butter in another saucepan and stir in the flour. Remove from heat and gradually add milk. Return to heat and bring to the boil, stirring until thickened. Remove from heat and stir in a pinch of nutmeg, egg yolks, cheese and seasoning.

Preheat the grill.

Lift out chicory with draining spoon. Reserve cooking liquor. Wrap each chicory head in a slice of ham and arrange in a greased ovenproof dish. Add reserved liquor to sauce, beat well, then pour over chicory. Dot with the rest of the butter and grill for 5–10 minutes till golden on top. Serve immediately.

Carrot soufflé

Overall timing 1 hour

Freezing Not suitable

To serve 4

1lb	Carrots	450g
2oz	Butter	50g
	Salt and pepper	
Sauce base		
2oz	Butter	50g
2oz	Plain flour	50g
1 pint	Milk	560ml
	Salt and pepper	
3	Eggs	3

Peel and thinly slice the carrots, then cook in boiling water for 15 minutes. Drain and plunge into cold water to cool carrots quickly.

Melt butter in another pan, add drained carrots and cook for 5 minutes. Season with salt and pepper.

Preheat oven to 375°F (190°C) Gas 5.

For the sauce base, melt butter in a saucepan and stir in flour. Gradually add milk and bring to the boil, stirring until thickened. Season with salt and pepper and cool.

Separate the eggs. Mix the egg yolks and carrots into the sauce. Whisk the whites in a bowl until very stiff, then carefully fold into the carrot mixture. Pour into a greased 3 pint (1.7 litre) soufflé dish. Bake for about 30 minutes until the soufflé is golden and well risen. Serve immediately.

Bean gratin

Overall timing 40 minutes

Freezing Not suitable

To serve 6

2 oz	Bread	50 g
	Milk	
1	Garlic clove	1
1 tbsp	Chopped parsley	15 ml
8 oz	Leftover cooked lamb or beef	225 g
	Salt and pepper	
2x14 oz	Cans of green beans *or*	2x397 g
1 lb	Frozen beans *or*	450 g
$1\frac{1}{4}$ lb	Fresh cooked beans	600 g
1 oz	Butter	25 g
1 oz	Plain flour	25 g
$\frac{3}{4}$ pint	Milk	400 ml
3 oz	Cheese	75 g
1	Egg	1

Preheat oven to 450°F (230°C) Gas 8.

Soak the bread in a little milk. Squeeze out, then put through a mincer with the peeled garlic, parsley and meat. Season with salt and pepper.

If using canned beans, drain them. Fill a well-greased gratin dish with alternate layers of beans and meat mixture, finishing with a bean layer.

Melt butter in a saucepan. Stir in flour and cook for 1 minute, then gradually add milk. Bring to the boil, stirring until thickened. Grate cheese and add to sauce. Cool slightly, then mix in beaten egg and seasoning.

Cover bean mixture in gratin dish with the sauce. Bake for about 10 minutes until the sauce is lightly browned.

Lettuce and ham supper

Overall timing 40 minutes

Freezing Not suitable

To serve 4

4	Round lettuces	4
1	Onion	1
1 oz	Butter	25 g
½ pint	Chicken stock	300 ml
	Salt and pepper	
4	Thick slices of cooked ham	4
1 teasp	Cornflour	5 ml
2 tbsp	Water	2x15 ml
¼ pint	Sherry	150 ml

Trim and wash lettuces. Drain well and cut in half lengthways. Peel and chop the onion.

Melt the butter in a saucepan and fry onions till golden. Add lettuces and fry for 3 minutes. Add stock, salt and pepper. Tightly cover pan and simmer gently for 15–20 minutes.

Cut ham slices in half and add to pan. Heat through gently for 3 minutes.

Carefully lift out the lettuce halves and ham, draining thoroughly. Arrange on a warmed serving dish and keep hot.

Blend cornflour with water, then stir into cooking liquor. Bring to the boil, stirring continuously. Remove from heat and stir in sherry. Taste and adjust seasoning. Pour over lettuce and ham and serve immediately with mashed potatoes and wholemeal bread.

Mushrooms in batter

Overall timing 30 minutes

Freezing Not suitable

To serve 2–4

12 oz	Large open mushrooms	350 g
$4\frac{1}{2}$ oz	Plain flour	140 g
1 teasp	Salt	5 ml
1	Egg	1
1 tbsp	Oil	15 ml
$\frac{1}{4}$ pint	Milk or water	150 ml
2	Egg whites	2
	Oil for frying	
	Sprigs of parsley	

Trim the mushrooms, then toss in $\frac{1}{2}$ oz (15 g) of the flour.

Sift the remaining flour and salt into a bowl and make a well in the centre. Add the egg and oil and begin to mix with a wooden spoon, drawing the flour into the liquid. Gradually stir in the milk or water to make a thick smooth batter. Whisk the egg whites in a bowl till stiff but not dry and fold gently into the batter.

Heat oil in a deep-fryer to 340°F (170°C).

Spear a mushroom on a long skewer and dip into the batter. Using a second skewer, carefully push the mushroom off the skewer into the oil. Fry the mushrooms, a few at a time, for 3–4 minutes till crisp and golden. Remove from the pan with a draining spoon and drain on kitchen paper. Pile on to a warmed serving plate and garnish with sprigs of parsley.

Cabbage parcels

Overall timing $1\frac{1}{4}$ hours

Freezing Not suitable

To serve 4

1	White cabbage	1
3oz	Long grain rice	75g
1	Small onion	1
6 tbsp	Oil	6x15ml
8oz	Minced beef	225g
	Salt and pepper	
$\frac{1}{4}$ teasp	Grated nutmeg	1.25ml
1 teasp	Dried oregano	5ml
8fl oz	Stock	220ml
1oz	Butter	25g
1 tbsp	Plain flour	15ml
1	Egg	1
2	Egg yolks	2
6 tbsp	Lemon juice	6x15ml
$\frac{3}{4}$ pint	White sauce	400ml

Remove core from cabbage and cook in boiling water for 5 minutes. Drain and cool, then peel away 16–20 leaves. Add rice to same pan of boiling water and cook till tender. Drain.

Peel and chop onion. Heat 4 tbsp (4x15ml) oil in a frying pan and cook onion till transparent. Add mince, salt, pepper, nutmeg and oregano. Cook for 5–8 minutes. Cool, then mix in rice.

Place a little stuffing on each cabbage leaf. Fold in sides and roll into tight parcels. Heat rest of oil in flameproof casserole. Pack cabbage rolls tightly in casserole and pour in stock. Cut leftover cabbage heart in two and place on top. Cover and simmer gently for 40 minutes.

Transfer cabbage rolls to warmed serving dish. Pour cooking liquor into a measuring jug and make up to 8fl oz (220ml) with water if necessary.

Melt butter in saucepan, then stir in flour and cooking liquor and simmer until thickened. Beat egg and egg yolks with lemon juice till foamy. Add to pan off heat. Return to a gentle heat. Don't allow sauce to boil. Stir in white sauce and heat. Pour sauce over rolls.

Lentils with bacon

Overall timing $1\frac{1}{2}$ hours

Freezing Suitable

To serve 4

8oz	Continental lentils	225g
1	Large onion	1
8oz	Smoked streaky bacon	225g
3 tbsp	Oil	3x15ml
1 teasp	Salt	5ml
3 tbsp	Tomato purée	3x15ml
$1\frac{1}{2}$ pints	Stock	850ml

Wash and pick over the lentils. Peel and finely chop the onion. Derind and dice the bacon. Heat oil in a saucepan and fry onion and bacon till golden. Add the lentils and salt and cook for 10 minutes, stirring frequently.

Stir in the tomato purée and the stock and simmer for about 1 hour until the lentils are tender. Taste and adjust seasoning. Serve on slices of fried bread with a mixed salad.

Spicy stuffed peppers

Overall timing $1\frac{1}{4}$ hours

Freezing Not suitable

To serve 4

8	Green or red peppers	8
	Salt and pepper	
1	Onion	1
2 tbsp	Oil	2x15 ml
1 lb	Minced beef	450 g
1 pint	Beef stock	560 ml
6 oz	Long grain rice	175 g
1 teasp	Grated nutmeg	5 ml
1 tbsp	Brown sugar	15 ml
2 oz	Cheese	50 g

Cut stalk ends off peppers and remove seeds and membrane. Blanch in boiling salted water for 5 minutes, then drain. Arrange in a greased ovenproof dish.

Peel and chop onion and pepper lids. Heat oil in a saucepan and fry onion and pepper lids till just golden. Add beef and brown well. Stir in stock and bring to the boil. Add rice, nutmeg, sugar and seasoning and simmer for 15–20 minutes till rice is tender and has absorbed the stock.

Remove from heat. Grate cheese and stir into stuffing. Use to fill the peppers. Cover the dish with foil and bake for 20 minutes. Remove foil and bake for a further 10 minutes till golden.

Stuffed baked turnips

Overall timing $1\frac{1}{4}$ hours

Freezing Not suitable

To serve 4

4x8 oz	Turnips	4x225 g
	Salt and pepper	
1	Onion	1
1 oz	Butter	25 g
2 oz	Fresh breadcrumbs	50 g
8 oz	Sliced cooked ham	225 g
1	Egg yolk	1
$\frac{1}{4}$ pint	Chicken stock	150 ml
3 oz	Cheese	75 g

Preheat the oven to 375°F (190°C) Gas 5.

Peel turnips. Cut off top third of each to make a lid. Scoop flesh out of base, leaving a thick shell, and chop flesh. Cook shells and lids in boiling salted water for 5 minutes, then drain.

Peel and chop onion. Melt butter in a saucepan, add onion and chopped turnip and fry till golden. Stir in breadcrumbs. Reserve four slices of ham, chop rest and add to stuffing with seasoning and egg yolk.

Press stuffing into turnips. Place a slice of ham on each and cover with lids. Put in ovenproof dish. Pour stock over, cover and bake for 20 minutes.

Grate cheese. Uncover turnips, sprinkle over cheese and bake for a further 10–15 minutes.

Sausagemeat tomatoes

Overall timing 45 minutes

Freezing Not suitable

To serve 4		
8	Tomatoes	8
1	Large onion	1
4 tbsp	Oil	4x15 ml
12 oz	Pork sausagemeat	350 g
2 oz	Fresh breadcrumbs	50 g
1 tbsp	Chopped parsley	15 ml
	Salt and pepper	
1	Egg	1

Preheat the oven to 350°F (180°C) Gas 4.

Cut lids off the tomatoes and scoop out the flesh. Discard the seeds and chop the flesh. Peel and chop onion. Heat half the oil in a frying pan and fry onion till transparent. Add sausagemeat and fry until browned.

Remove from heat and stir in tomato flesh, breadcrumbs, parsley and seasoning. Bind with egg. Press mixture into tomato shells and replace lids.

Arrange tomatoes in ovenproof dish and brush with remaining oil. Bake for 30 minutes. Serve hot.

Lamb-stuffed onions

Overall timing $1\frac{1}{4}$ hours

Freezing Not suitable

To serve 6		
6	Large onions	6
	Salt and pepper	
2 tbsp	Oil	2x15 ml
$1\frac{1}{2}$ teasp	Mixed spice	7.5 ml
1 lb	Minced lamb	450 g
1 oz	Fresh breadcrumbs	25 g
4 oz	Cottage cheese	125 g
1 oz	Butter	25 g
2 tbsp	Plain flour	2x15 ml
3 tbsp	Tomato purée	3x15 ml
$\frac{1}{2}$ pint	Light stock	300 ml

Peel onions and cook in boiling salted water for 15 minutes. Drain and cool. Remove slice from bottom of each onion. Cut slice from top and scoop out centres, leaving a $\frac{1}{2}$ inch (12.5mm) shell. Put shells in flameproof casserole. Chop onion centres.

Heat oil and fry chopped onion with spice for 3 minutes. Add lamb and fry for 5 minutes. Stir in breadcrumbs, cheese and seasoning. Press into onion shells.

Melt butter, add flour and stir in tomato purée, stock and seasoning. Bring to the boil and pour over onions. Cover and simmer for 45 minutes till onions are tender.

Roman macaroni soup

Overall timing 1 hour 50 minutes

Freezing Not suitable

To serve 6

8 oz	Piece of pork rind	225 g
2 pints	Stock	1.1 litres
	Bouquet garni	
1	Large cauliflower	1
	Salt and pepper	
1	Onion	1
1	Garlic clove	1
1 tbsp	Oil	15 ml
4 oz	Sliced cooked ham	125 g
8 oz	Long macaroni	225 g
2 oz	Cheese	50 g

Scrape pork rind and singe off any bristles. Wipe with a damp cloth and cut into pieces. Place pork in a saucepan with stock and bouquet garni and boil for 1 hour. Alternatively, cut rind into strips, rub with salt and oil and cook on baking tray in 425°F (220°C) Gas 7 oven for 30 minutes till crisp.

Meanwhile, trim cauliflower and divide into florets. Cook in boiling salted water for 5 minutes. Drain.

Peel and chop onion; peel and crush garlic. Heat oil in a flameproof casserole, add onion and garlic and fry for 5 minutes. Cut ham into thin strips, add to pan and fry for 5 minutes.

Drain pork rind and add to casserole with 1¾ pints (1 litre) of the cooking liquor (discard bouquet garni). Bring to the boil.

Break macaroni into 2 inch (5 cm) pieces. Add to casserole with pinch of salt and simmer till tender. Add cauliflower and simmer for another minute. Taste and adjust seasoning. Serve immediately with grated cheese.

Savoury dumpling soup

Overall timing 2½ hours

Freezing Suitable: add dumplings after reheating

To serve 6–8

1	Onion	1
4 oz	Carrots	125 g
3 oz	Parsnips	75 g
5	Stalks of celery	5
3 oz	Butter	75 g
2 tbsp	Plain flour	2x15 ml
3 pints	Chicken stock	1.7 litres
1 lb	Cooked chicken joints	450 g
Dumplings		
4 oz	Fresh breadcrumbs	125 g
2 oz	Streaky bacon	50 g
4 oz	Calf's liver	125 g
4 oz	Minced beef	125 g
1	Onion	1
1	Egg	1
½ teasp	Dried marjoram	2.5 ml
	Salt and pepper	
1 tbsp	Chopped parsley	15 ml

First make dumplings. Soak breadcrumbs in ½ pint (300 ml) water for 15 minutes. Derind and chop bacon and fry till crisp. Mince liver. Add beef, squeezed out breadcrumbs, chopped onion, drained bacon, egg, marjoram, seasoning and parsley. Shape into small dumplings.

Peel and chop onion, carrots and parsnips; chop celery. Melt butter, add onions and cook for 2–3 minutes. Add carrots, celery and parsnips, cover and cook till tender. Sieve vegetables and return to pan. Stir in flour then 1 pint (560 ml) stock. Simmer until thickened. Add remaining stock.

Skin, bone and chop chicken. Add to soup with dumplings and simmer for 15 minutes.

American fish chowder

Overall timing $1\frac{1}{2}$ hours

Freezing Suitable

To serve 4

2lb	Mixed white fish	900g
2oz	Streaky bacon	50g
1 tbsp	Oil	15ml
1	Large onion	1
4	Medium potatoes	4
4	Carrots	4
4	Stalks of celery	4
1 tbsp	Chopped parsley	15ml
14oz	Can of tomatoes	397g
$1\frac{1}{2}$ pints	Fish stock or water	850ml
2 tbsp	Tomato ketchup	2x15ml
2 tbsp	Worcestershire sauce	2x15ml
	Dried thyme	
	Salt and pepper	

Skin and bone fish and cut into bite-size pieces. Derind and dice bacon.

Heat oil in a saucepan and fry bacon till crisp. Remove from pan. Peel and chop onion and add to pan. Cook gently till transparent.

Peel and chop potatoes and carrots. Finely chop celery. Add to pan with chopped parsley, tomatoes and their juice, fish stock or water, tomato ketchup, Worcestershire sauce, a pinch of thyme and seasoning. Cover and simmer gently for about 45 minutes.

Add the fish pieces and bacon, cover and cook for a further 15 minutes.

Turkish soup with meatballs

Overall timing 1¾ hours

Freezing Not suitable

To serve 4–6

1	Knuckle of veal	1
1 lb	Shin of beef	450 g
1	Large onion	1
2	Large carrots	2
1	Stalk of celery	1
	Parsley stalks	
	Salt and pepper	
2	Eggs	2
3 tbsp	Lemon juice	3x15 ml
Meatballs		
1 lb	Minced beef	450 g
4 oz	Cooked long grain rice	125 g
1	Egg	1
1 tbsp	Chopped parsley	15 ml
¼ teasp	Grated nutmeg	1.25 ml
	Salt and pepper	
1 oz	Butter	25 g
2 tbsp	Oil	2x15 ml

Chop knuckle in half lengthways. Dice beef. Peel and chop onion and carrots; chop celery. Put meat and vegetables into a saucepan with 4 pints (2.2 litres) water, parsley stalks and seasoning. Cover and simmer for 45 minutes.

Meanwhile, mix beef with rice, egg, parsley, nutmeg and seasoning to a stiff paste and shape into small balls.

Heat butter and oil in a frying pan. Add meatballs and fry till browned all over.

Strain stock, discarding meat and vegetables. Return to pan and bring back to boil. Add meatballs and simmer for 15 minutes.

Put the eggs and lemon juice into a tureen and gradually stir in soup.

Majorcan vegetable and bread soup

Overall timing $1\frac{1}{2}$ hours

Freezing Not suitable

To serve 6

8 oz	Continental lentils	225 g
3 pints	Water	1.7 litres
4 oz	Streaky bacon rashers	125 g
1 lb	Fresh broad beans	450 g
1 lb	Fresh peas	450 g
1 lb	Cabbage	450 g
8 oz	Fresh spinach	225 g
	Salt and pepper	
18	Thin slices of brown bread	18

Wash and pick over the lentils and put into a saucepan with the water. Bring to the boil and simmer for 45 minutes.

Meanwhile, derind and dice the bacon. Shell the beans and peas. Shred the cabbage and spinach.

Rub the lentils with their cooking liquor through a sieve or purée in a blender. Return to the saucepan and add seasoning, bacon and vegetables and bring to the boil. Simmer for about 25 minutes till the vegetables are tender.

Taste and adjust the seasoning. Arrange three slices of bread in each soup bowl and pour the soup over. Serve immediately.

Minestrone col pesto

Overall timing $2\frac{1}{2}$ hours plus soaking

Freezing Suitable: add pesto after reheating

To serve 8

4oz	Dried kidney beans	125g
1	Onion	1
1	Garlic clove	1
3 tbsp	Oil	3x15ml
2 tbsp	Chopped parsley	2x15ml
8oz	Head of celery	225g
4oz	Spinach	125g
4oz	Cabbage	125g
4oz	Carrots	125g
12oz	Tomatoes	350g
4oz	Courgettes	125g
11oz	Potatoes	300g
8oz	Fresh or frozen peas	225g
1 tbsp	Salt	15ml
6oz	Spaghetti	175g
	Pesto (see page 27)	

Soak beans in water to cover for 2 hours.

Peel and chop onion; peel and crush garlic. Heat oil and fry onion, garlic and parsley for 3 minutes. Set aside.

Chop celery and spinach. Shred cabbage. Scrape and slice carrots. Blanch, peel and chop tomatoes. Dice courgettes; peel and dice potatoes. If using fresh peas, shell them.

Bring $4\frac{1}{2}$ pints (2.5 litres) water to the boil in a large saucepan. Add salt and vegetables, including those fried, and drained beans. (If using frozen peas do not add yet.) Cover and simmer for $1\frac{1}{2}$ hours.

Break spaghetti into short lengths and add to soup with frozen peas, if used. Stir, then continue simmering for 15 minutes.

Stir pesto into soup and simmer for a few more minutes.

Swiss cream of barley soup

Overall timing $2\frac{3}{4}$ hours

Freezing Not suitable

To serve 4–6

2	Large onions	2
3	Cloves	3
1	Calf's foot	1
4 oz	Pearl barley	125 g
	Bay leaf	
3 pints	Water	1.7 litres
	Salt and pepper	
12 oz	Carrots	350 g
4	Stalks of celery	4
2	Small leeks	2
4 oz	Smoked streaky bacon rashers	125 g
2 oz	Lard	50 g
2	Egg yolks	2
$\frac{1}{4}$ pint	Carton of single cream	150 ml
1 tbsp	Chopped chives	15 ml

Peel one of the onions and spike with cloves. Wash calf's foot, chop in half lengthways and put into a saucepan with the barley, spiked onion and bay leaf. Add the water and seasoning, then cover and simmer for 2 hours.

Meanwhile, scrape and dice carrots. Peel and chop remaining onion. Trim and chop celery and leeks. Derind and dice bacon. Melt lard in a large saucepan. Add bacon and vegetables and fry for 10 minutes till golden.

Remove spiked onion and bay leaf from stock and discard. Lift calf's foot out of stock and remove the meat, discarding skin and bones. Add meat to stock with the vegetables. Bring to the boil and simmer for 10 minutes till vegetables are tender.

Put the egg yolks and cream into a tureen and beat together with a fork. Season the soup to taste and gradually stir into tureen. Sprinkle with chives and serve.

Tuscan vegetable soup

Overall timing 2 hours plus overnight soaking

Freezing Not suitable

To serve 6

8 oz	Dried beans	225 g
$1\frac{1}{4}$ lb	Cabbage	600 g
1	Onion	1
1	Large leek	1
1	Stalk of celery	1
1	Carrot	1
1	Garlic clove	1
3 tbsp	Oil	3x15 ml
1	Bay leaf	1
3	Sprigs of oregano	3
	Sprig of rosemary	
	Salt and pepper	
2 tbsp	Tomato purée	2x15 ml
3 pints	Light stock	1.7 litres

Soak beans in cold water overnight. The next day, drain beans, put into a large saucepan and cover with fresh cold water. Bring to the boil and simmer for about $1\frac{1}{2}$ hours till tender.

Meanwhile, shred cabbage. Peel and thinly slice onion; trim and slice leek and celery. Scrape and chop carrot. Peel and crush garlic. Heat oil in a large saucepan and fry vegetables, except cabbage, with garlic and herbs till lightly browned. Add cabbage and seasoning and fry for a further 5 minutes.

Remove herbs from pan and add the tomato purée, drained beans and stock. Bring to the boil and simmer for a further 15 minutes. Taste and adjust the seasoning and pour into warmed individual bowls.

Tongue salad

Overall timing 1 hour

Freezing Not suitable

To serve 4

1 lb	New potatoes	450 g
3	Small onions	3
$\frac{1}{2}$	Cucumber	$\frac{1}{2}$
$7\frac{1}{2}$ oz	Can of button mushrooms	212 g
4	Hard-boiled eggs	4
8 oz	Sliced cooked tongue	225 g
4 tbsp	Wine vinegar	4x15 ml
6 tbsp	Oil	6x15 ml
	Salt and pepper	
2 tbsp	Chopped fresh herbs	2x15 ml
4 fl oz	Cold beef stock	120 ml

Cook the potatoes in boiling salted water for about 15 minutes till tender. Drain, peel and slice thickly into a bowl.

Peel and thinly slice onions into rings and add to the bowl. Thinly slice cucumber; drain mushrooms. Shell eggs and cut lengthways into quarters; cut tongue into strips. Add all to the potatoes and mix carefully.

Put the vinegar, oil, seasoning and herbs into a screw-top jar. Shake well, then pour over the salad and mix lightly. Chill for 15 minutes.

Add the stock, mix lightly and serve.

Kipper salad

Overall timing 20 minutes

Freezing Not suitable

To serve 4

4	Kipper fillets	4
4	Cold boiled potatoes	4
1	Cooked beetroot	1
1 tbsp	Chopped onion	15 ml
8 tbsp	Mayonnaise	8x15 ml
	Sprigs of parsley	

Place kippers upright in a jug, fill with boiling water and leave for 5 minutes. Drain, pat dry with kitchen paper, then chop into pieces. Cube potatoes and beetroot.

Put kippers, potatoes, beetroot and onion in salad bowl. Mix well. Spoon mayonnaise over and garnish with parsley sprigs.

Apple and salami salad

Overall timing 40 minutes

Freezing Not suitable

To serve 4

3	Small onions	3
3	Apples	3
8oz	Salami	225g
2	Large gherkins	2
1 tbsp	Vinegar	15ml
1 tbsp	Lemon juice	15ml
3 tbsp	Oil	3x15ml
	Salt and pepper	
	Pinch of caster sugar	
$\frac{1}{4}$ teasp	Celery or mustard seeds	1.25ml

Peel onions and cut into thin rings. Peel, core and chop apples. Dice salami and gherkins. Put them all in a salad bowl and mix well together.

Combine all remaining ingredients to make the dressing and pour over salad, mixing it in well. Leave for 20 minutes to blend the flavours before serving, with crusty bread and butter.

Buckling and potato salad

Overall timing 30 minutes

Freezing Not suitable

To serve 4–6

3	Buckling	3
8oz	Cold boiled potatoes	225g
8oz	Red apples	225g
2	Tomatoes	2
2	Hard-boiled eggs	2
	Sprig of dill or fennel	
Dressing		
4 tbsp	Olive oil	4x15ml
3 tbsp	Lemon juice	3x15ml
	Salt and pepper	

Slice buckling along backbone. Skin and fillet, then blanch in boiling water for 3 minutes. Break fish into large pieces and place in serving bowl.

Cut the potatoes into cubes and add to bowl. Core and dice apples. Add to fish and potatoes.

Mix the olive oil, lemon juice and seasoning together to make a dressing. Pour over the fish mixture. Toss carefully and leave for 15 minutes for the flavours to develop.

Wash tomatoes and cut into eighths. Shell and slice eggs and arrange with the tomatoes and herbs around the salad. Serve with hot, crusty bread.

Asparagus and ham salad

Overall timing 20 minutes plus chilling

Freezing Not suitable

To serve 4

12oz	Can of asparagus spears	340g
4oz	Cooked ham	125g
4	Pineapple rings	4
	Lettuce leaves	
8 tbsp	Mayonnaise	8x15ml
½ teasp	Brandy (optional)	2.5ml
2 tbsp	Lemon juice	2x15ml
	Pinch of cayenne	
Garnish		
2	Tomatoes	2
2	Hard-boiled eggs	2
	Chopped parsley	

Drain and chop asparagus and place in a mixing bowl. Dice ham. Chop the pineapple rings. Add both to asparagus and mix together well.

Place lettuce in the bottom of individual glasses. Divide asparagus mixture evenly between them.

Mix mayonnaise with brandy, if using, lemon juice and cayenne. Divide dressing equally between glasses. Garnish with chopped tomato, sliced hard-boiled egg and chopped parsley. Chill for 10 minutes before serving.

Russian salad

Overall timing 30 minutes

Freezing Not suitable

To serve 4

3	Medium potatoes	3
2	Carrots	2
4oz	Green beans	125g
2	Stalks of celery	2
	Salt and pepper	
4oz	Frozen peas	125g
2 tbsp	Capers	2x15ml
	Juice of $\frac{1}{2}$ lemon	
8fl oz	Carton of double cream	227ml
2	Hard-boiled eggs	2

Peel and dice potatoes and carrots. Top and tail beans and remove strings. Cut beans into small pieces. Trim and finely dice celery.

Place potatoes in boiling salted water and cook for 5 minutes. Remove with draining spoon, place in colander and rinse under cold water. Add carrots to pan and cook for 5 minutes. Remove and rinse. Add beans, peas and celery to pan and cook for 4 minutes. Remove and rinse.

Drain cooled vegetables and place in bowl with capers. Add lemon juice and salt and pepper. Pour cream over and mix carefully. Pile salad on to a serving plate.

Shell and quarter eggs and arrange round the edge of the plate.

Hot frankfurter salad

Overall timing 45 minutes

Freezing Not suitable

To serve 4

1lb	Waxy potatoes	450g
	Salt and pepper	
4	Frankfurters	4
2	Onions	2
4	Anchovy fillets	4
2oz	Chopped gherkins	50g
2 tbsp	Oil	2x15ml
2 tbsp	White wine vinegar	2x15ml

Peel and slice potatoes, then cook in boiling salted water for about 7 minutes till tender.

Heat frankfurters in boiling water for 5 minutes, then drain and slice. Peel and slice onions into rings. Finely chop anchovies and gherkins. Drain potatoes and mix with frankfurters and onions.

Beat together oil and vinegar, season and pour over the warm salad. Mix well and leave for 10 minutes. Add anchovies and gherkins and serve.

Tuna rolls

Overall timing 15 minutes

Freezing Not suitable

To serve 4

4	Long rolls	4
	Butter	
	Mayonnaise	
1x7oz	Can of tuna fish	1x200g
	Chopped parsley	
2	Hard-boiled eggs	2
	Radish roses	

Halve the rolls, not cutting all the way through, and butter the cut surfaces. Spread a thick layer of mayonnaise over the bottom cut surface.

Drain the tuna and flake it. Divide between the rolls and sprinkle with parsley. Arrange the sandwiches on a serving plate.

Shell and slice the eggs and use to garnish the sandwiches with radish roses.

Broccoli toasts

Overall timing 40 minutes

Freezing Not suitable

To serve 4

1 lb	Calabrese broccoli	450 g
½ pint	Beef stock	300 ml
8	Slices of bread	8
½ pint	Thick white sauce	300 ml
	Salt and pepper	
	Grated nutmeg	
½ teasp	Mixed herbs	2.5 ml
2	Hard-boiled eggs	2
1	Tomato	1
	Sprigs of parsley	
½	Red pepper	½

Trim broccoli and chop into large pieces. Bring stock to boil, add broccoli and cook for 7–10 minutes.

Toast bread and place on baking tray. Drain broccoli well, then divide it between toast.

Preheat oven to 375°F (190°C) Gas 5.

Heat sauce, then add seasoning, pinch of nutmeg and herbs. Finely chop one of the hard-boiled eggs and add to the sauce. Pour sauce over broccoli. Bake for 15 minutes.

Serve hot, garnished with remaining egg, sliced tomato, parsley and strips of pepper.

Pirozski

Overall timing 1 hour

Freezing Suitable: refresh in 350°F (180°C) Gas 4 oven for 10 minutes

To serve 6

7½ oz	Frozen puff pastry	212 g
8 oz	Liver pâté	225 g
1	Egg	1

Thaw pastry. Preheat the oven to 400°F (200°C) Gas 6.

Roll out dough very thinly on a floured surface and cut into 3 inch (7.5 cm) squares. Cut in half diagonally to make triangles. Put about 1 teasp (5 ml) liver pâté on half of the triangles. Moisten dough edges and cover with remaining triangles. Press edges together to seal.

Arrange triangles on greased baking tray and brush with beaten egg. Bake for 10–15 minutes till well risen and golden. Serve hot.

Egg and cheese sandwiches

Overall timing 30 minutes

Freezing Not suitable

To serve 4

1	Small onion	1
4oz	Butter	125g
2oz	Mushrooms	50g
4 tbsp	Dry white wine	4x15ml
4 tbsp	Chicken stock	4x15ml
	Salt and pepper	
4oz	Cooked ham	125g
6oz	Cheddar cheese	175g
8	Slices of bread	8
	Paprika	
4	Eggs	4

Peel and finely chop onion. Melt 1oz (25g) of the butter in a pan and cook onion till transparent. Slice mushrooms, add to pan and cook for 3 minutes. Add wine and stock and cook over a high heat until most of the liquid evaporates. Season with salt and pepper.

Preheat the oven to 400°F (200°C) Gas 6.

Cut the ham and cheese into thin slices. Butter the bread and place four slices in a shallow ovenproof dish, buttered side down. Divide cheese, ham, mushrooms and onion between them and sprinkle with a little paprika. Cover with remaining bread slices, buttered side up. Bake for 10 minutes until crisp and golden.

Meanwhile, melt remaining butter in a frying pan. Break eggs one at a time into a cup, then slide into the pan when butter is frothy. Cook for 2–3 minutes. Remove eggs from pan with an egg slice. Place on top of sandwiches, sprinkle with salt and pepper and serve.

Welsh rarebit

Overall timing 30 minutes

Freezing Not suitable

To serve 4		
8	Slices of bread	8
3oz	Butter	75g
12oz	Cheddar cheese	350g
½ teasp	Ground mace	2.5ml
	Pinch of powdered mustard	
5 tbsp	Beer	5x15ml
	Pepper	

Preheat the oven to 400°F (200°C) Gas 6.

Toast the bread, and butter the slices while still hot. Place on baking tray.

Cut the cheese into small cubes and put in a saucepan with mace, mustard and beer. Cook over a low heat, stirring with a wooden spoon, until cheese melts and is thick and creamy. Spread mixture over toast. Sprinkle generously with pepper and bake for 10 minutes. Serve immediately.

Deep-fried Mozzarella sandwiches

Overall timing 20 minutes

Freezing Not suitable

To serve 4

8	Slices of bread	8
4	Slices of Mozzarella cheese	4
	Plain flour	
1	Egg	1
	Oil for deep frying	

Remove the crusts from the bread. Make four sandwiches with the cheese and coat all over with flour. Beat the egg in a shallow dish. Dip in the sandwiches so the sides and edges are all coated.

Heat oil in a deep-fryer to 360°F (180°C). Deep fry the sandwiches until they are golden brown. Drain on kitchen paper and serve hot, with salad.

Croque monsieur

Overall timing 20 minutes

Freezing Not suitable

To serve 4

8	Slices of bread	8
	Butter	
8	Slices of Gruyère or Cheddar cheese	8
4	Slices of cooked ham	4
	Extra grated cheese (optional)	

Preheat the grill.

Butter four slices of bread. Place a slice of cheese on each of the unbuttered slices of bread. Cover with the ham, then top with the rest of the sliced cheese. Place the buttered bread on top, buttered sides up.

Grill the sandwiches, buttered sides up, until golden brown. Turn and spread the other sides with butter. Continue grilling until golden. Sprinkle with a little extra grated cheese, if liked, and grill until the cheese has melted.

Variation

For a Croque milady, add sliced tomato to the sandwich and top with fried eggs.

Provençal sandwiches

Overall timing 15 minutes

Freezing Not suitable

To serve 4

4	Crusty rolls	4
1	Garlic clove	1
4	Large lettuce leaves	4
2	Large tomatoes	2
2	Hard-boiled eggs	2
	Pickled vegetables or gherkins	
	Black olives	
	Cooked green beans	
	Anchovy fillets	
	Green or red pepper	
	Olive oil	
	Vinegar	

Halve the rolls and the garlic clove. Rub the cut surfaces of the rolls with the garlic. Place the lettuce leaves on the bottom halves of the rolls.

Slice the tomatoes. Shell and slice the eggs. Place the tomatoes and eggs on the lettuce, then add pickled vegetables or gherkins, olives, beans, anchovies and pepper strips, according to taste. Sprinkle with oil and vinegar, then place the tops of the rolls on the filling. Press gently together and serve.

Sausage in brioche

Overall timing $2\frac{1}{2}$ hours plus rising

Freezing Not suitable

To serve 6–8

1lb	Piece of fresh continental sausage	450g
	Bouquet garni	
1	Onion	1
8oz	Strong flour	225g
$\frac{1}{4}$ teasp	Salt	1.25ml
$1\frac{1}{2}$ teasp	Dried yeast	7.5ml
2 tbsp	Lukewarm water	2x15ml
1 tbsp	Caster sugar	15ml
2	Eggs	2
2oz	Butter	50g
1	Egg yolk	1

Put sausage into a saucepan with bouquet garni and peeled onion and cover with cold water. Bring to the boil and simmer very gently for $1\frac{3}{4}$ hours.

Meanwhile, sift flour and salt into a bowl. Sprinkle yeast on to the water, add a pinch of the sugar and mix well. Leave in a warm place till frothy, then add to flour with remaining sugar. Add eggs and melted butter to flour and mix to a soft dough. Knead till glossy, wrap in oiled polythene and leave in a warm place to rise.

Drain sausage, discarding flavourings, and allow to cool slightly. Remove the skin.

Preheat the oven to 425°F (220°C) Gas 7.

Roll out dough to a rectangle large enough to enclose the sausage. Place sausage in centre and fold dough round it, pinching edges to seal. Place, join down, on a baking tray. Leave to prove for 15 minutes.

Brush with beaten egg yolk and bake for about 25 minutes till crisp and golden. Serve hot, cut into thick slices.

Index